A FAMILY'S LOVE . . .
A FAMILY'S LOSS

Our lawyer Saul squinted as his eyes adjusted from the sun to the dark restaurant. We waved and he came to our table. He looked pale as he sat down. "Sorry I'm late," he said. "I was held up in court. Jesus, he's beautiful," he said, stroking Chris's cheek.

"Isn't he great?" said Jeremy.

"We're real happy," I smiled. "When is the consent signing?"

"I'm so sorry," said Saul. He fingered the tines of his fork.

"Why? What's the matter?"

"She won't sign anything. She wants him."

"What?"

"She wants him."

"What do you mean, Saul?" Christopher started squirming. I stuck a bottle in his mouth and he sucked.

"I just hate to be here. I hate this," he said. "Her lawyer called me. She told him she changed her mind. There isn't going to be a consent. She wants the kid."

Adoption Story:

A Son Is Given

Marguerite Ryan

LEISURE BOOKS   NEW YORK CITY

A LEISURE BOOK®

This edition is reprinted by arrangement with RAWSON ASSOCIATES, an imprint of Macmillan Publishing Company.

Published by

Dorchester Publishing Co., Inc.
276 Fifth Avenue
New York, NY 10001

For further information, contact: RAWSON ASSOCIATES, an imprint of Macmillan Publishing Company, 866 Third Avenue, New York, NY 10022.

The name "Leisure Books" and the stylized "L" with design are trademarks of Dorchester Publishing Co., Inc.

Printed in the United States of America.

Author's Note: Although this is a true story, the names have been changed to protect the privacy of those involved.

Adoption Story

CHAPTER
One

It was dark for lunch, but Christopher didn't seem to mind. I bounced him up and down on my lap, and he chortled at his reflection in the mirrors of the black-walled, candlelit restaurant. His laugh came from deep in his throat and sounded like a pigeon cooing. He was big for three months. Black straight hair grew down over his ears; the bangs almost covered his black-brown eyes. "We are very lucky," I said to Jeremy. "This is a special child."

Saul was late, so we went ahead and ordered. Christopher was patient, but a small baby might shift gears and erupt at any moment.

"There are two kinds of mothers," my sister had informed me, "ones that take their kids everywhere with them and ones that don't." I seemed to be the taking-with kind. Christopher had been to a pizza parlor at three days old, on a transcontinental flight at five days, to see *Peter Pan* on Broadway at twelve days. We'd visited out-of-town grandparents and squeezed in a yearly weekend reunion with four other couples before he was two months old.

He took these jaunts calmly, peering out from the Snugli or his flowered bassinet with those enormous liquid eyes. He was a self-contained little fellow, retiring and rising at 8:00, interrupting each evening's sleep only to have a bottle at about 3:00 A.M., a quick rock, then back to bed. Jeremy and I had absorbed this addition to our lives gratefully.

Saul squinted as his eyes adjusted from the sun to the dark restaurant. We waved and he came to our table. He looked pale as he sat down. "Sorry I'm late," he said. "I was held up in court. Jesus, he's beautiful," he said, stroking Chris's cheek.

"Isn't he great?" said Jeremy.

"We're real happy," I smiled. "When is the consent signing?"

"I'm so sorry," said Saul. He fingered the tines of his fork.

"Why? What's the matter?"

"She won't sign anything. She wants him."

"What?"

"She wants him."

"What do you mean, Saul?" Christopher started squirming. I stuck a bottle in his mouth and he sucked.

"I just hate to be here. I hate this," he said. "Her lawyer called me. She told him she changed her mind. There isn't going to be a consent. She wants the kid."

"Is that possible?" I said. "I mean, can she do that?" I looked from Jeremy to Saul and back to Jeremy. "Can she?"

Saul shrugged. "She can do anything she wants."

"What rights do we have?" Jeremy asked.

"Look guys, I'm really sorry." Saul picked up his knife, then slammed it down. "Jeremy, I don't know what to tell you. Legally, you're dead. She never signed a consent."

"But she signed that paper in the hospital," I said. My stomach ached, as if I'd swallowed a big lump of something that got stuck.

The waiter appeared with our food.

"I need a drink," Jeremy said. "Maggie, do you want something?"

"Scotch. On the rocks."

"She signed that paper, Saul," I repeated.

"It was only a placement-for-adoption paper," he said, "not an official consent."

"But Christopher is almost three months old. He's *our* baby."

Saul raised his palms in the air. "It stinks. It really stinks." A hairy, burly chested man, Saul squirmed in his chair. He seemed hampered by his three-piece suit.

Christopher had fallen asleep in the Snugli wrapped around my chest. His drool spread across the bib. His pink mouth opened in a tiny *O*. The laughter from other diners, the clatter of waiters clearing tables, had no effect on his need for a nap.

Jeremy said, "What are our options, Saul? How much time do we have?"

"A couple of days . . . a week, maybe," Saul answered.

I said, "Wait a minute. I'm sorry, but maybe I don't understand what's going on here." A rush of anger started to rise in my chest. "We were supposed to meet you here to discuss Angelina's consent. When did you know there was a problem?"

"Yesterday," said Saul. "Her lawyer called me from California yesterday."

"What does she think we've been doing for three months? Babysitting?"

"Maggie. Jeremy. I love you guys. I wanted this to

work, too. Listen," said Saul, "I'm starving. Are you going to eat that?" He pointed to my hamburger.

"No. Please have it." I pushed the plate over to him and gulped the rest of my Scotch. My chest burned as the alcohol went down, but my hands were ice cold.

"Saul, I'm trying to understand. Why did she wait until Christopher was three months old?"

Tears leaked from Jeremy's eyes. "Damn," he said. "Damn."

"What do we do?" I said to Jeremy. Jeremy was my rock. He took care of me, made big decisions easily, never seemed uncertain. This was only the second time I'd seen him cry. The first time had been at our wedding three years earlier.

"I don't know," he said. "But we're not giving him up."

"Jeremy. I'm not sure that you have a choice," said Saul.

"We're going to fight this," Jeremy said. "We're not giving Christopher up."

I was afraid. How did Jeremy know we *could* fight? Angelina, Angelina, what are you doing to us? Please, dear God, don't let this be real.

"Wait, remember, wasn't there a case like this in the seventies?" I said. "In New York, too. Baby Lenore, remember?"

"I dunno," said Saul dully. He'd eaten my hamburger too fast and looked very uncomfortable.

"The mother changed her mind, but she didn't get the baby back. I'm sure. They took the case to court. It was in all the papers."

"Maggie, we're going to talk to more lawyers," said Jeremy. "We're going to fight this." He put his hand over mine on the table. I looked into his eyes and was pained by the raw hurt I saw. Jeremy draws his chalk lines rather far from himself. He doesn't often let anyone get too close. It has taken me a long time, and frustrated me enormously, but I'm learning to respect his privacy. I've seen a look of love in his eyes, for me and for Christopher, that goes beyond words.

"I have to get some air," I said. "Jeremy, I want to go home. Can you come home with us now?" Jeremy's office was around the block, and afternoon appointments were waiting for him. But I didn't want to be alone.

We said an awkward good-bye to Saul and walked down Broadway. An aching man and woman and a sleeping baby. Christopher's breathing was regular and sure; his security intact. "She can't have you," I whispered to him. "You're mine. You're my baby doll."

"I have to call Eileen," I said when we got home. Eileen Conroy lived next door to the family in Marin County where Angelina worked as a live-in domestic. Eileen was fluent in Spanish and had an adopted daughter, two forces that had drawn Angelina to seek her counsel early in her pregnancy. I'd known Eileen years earlier in New York and had written to her for adoption advice at about the same time Angelina had approached her.

"Maggie, it's a tragedy, that's all I can say," wept Eileen. "I talked to Angelina on the phone this morning. She said she was not very good in her heart because of the baby.

"She can't study her English, she can't concentrate, she can't do anything. She wants to see the baby. I talked to her for a while and she seemed calmer. I told her it's not so simple anymore."

"Did you tell her you saw all three of us last week?" I asked. Eileen and her husband had been in New York on business and had come by to see Christopher. The evening had been festive, a cause for champagne and laughter and hearty toasts.

"Yes, I told her how happy you and Jeremy are, how good it is now. I told her about your appreciation toward her. I asked her not to try to turn things around. I asked her to consider this from a moral point of view."

"What did she say?"

"She cried. She referred to you as '*el matrimonal*,' the couple. She called you and Jeremy '*la señora*' and '*el señor*.' I told her that your hearts would be broken, and she said that her first decision had been almost a whim. That was the word she used. The Spanish word for that is *capricioso*."

"A whim," I said, shocked. "We're talking about a life."

"I know, Maggie. It is a shame. We left things at a standstill when she said that."

"A whim! God, that makes me furious," I said.

"I am very angry with Angelina," said Eileen.

"Should I come out there, Eileen? Do you think she would talk to me?"

"She needs somebody to help her get through this stage, Maggie. Maybe Father Ramo. It could be religious. She has to work through the guilt. She has to get back to the realities of what you and Jeremy have and can offer Christopher."

"So maybe Father Ramo should talk to her—not me." In my heart I was afraid to meet Angelina. And I couldn't take Christopher with me. But I couldn't leave him with anyone; he'd never even had a babysitter. And Jeremy had to work.

"Yes," said Eileen, "she needs to be talked to. She needs some concrete things to do to get her mind off dwelling over the baby. I told her she has everything that she wanted: the luxury of a private adoption, the satisfaction and assurance that he is loved and wanted and will be well taken care of."

"What did she say to that?" I asked. My head began to ache from all the talk.

"She kept talking about 'my son.' She cried a lot. I think she feels she's lost part of herself."

"Eileen, she's never even seen Christopher. He's been with us since day one. She's a complete stranger to him."

"Maggie," said Eileen, "perhaps she wants him to love her because she's lonely."

"I don't know what she wants," I said. "We want him for himself, not for what he can do for us. I just can't believe she would change her mind now."

"She's confused," said Eileen. "Maybe she needs some type of crisis intervention, like a mental health clinic."

"I think Father Ramo would be better," I said. "I mean, she knows him. He visited her in the hospital. She trusts him, right?"

"Yes, I think you're right. Do you want me to call him and ask him to call her?" asked Eileen.

"Would you, Eileen? I'm sorry to put you in the middle of this."

"Maggie, it's all right. I introduced you to this situation. I feel responsible."

"No, Eileen, please. It's not your fault. Who would have thought Angelina would change her mind? Maybe we didn't pay enough attention to her."

"Well, I never thought she should go back to that boarding house on Carmine Street," said Eileen, "where the father and his sister live. The sister probably gave her the idea to change her mind. Remember when she threw that baby shower for Angelina?"

The father's sister had not wanted the adoption, although her brother signed a consent and was satisfied with the plan.

"Yes, but Angelina wasn't bothered by the shower. She stayed with her decision."

"But she's so needy now," said Eileen. "She needs help from people who are supportive of her decision."

"What would she do with Christopher if she got him?" I asked.

"Where would she get money for food?" Eileen said. "The realities have to be spelled out."

"She can't even get welfare, can she?" I asked. "She's an illegal alien."

"That's another thing," said Eileen. "Christopher was born in California; that makes him an American citizen. Maybe that's why she wants him—to get a green card?"

"Oh God," I sighed.

"She's going to stop by tomorrow night on her way to work," said Eileen. "Maybe I can do a quick intervention then."

My head was reeling. Maybe this trouble would go away if we didn't tell anybody—if we just went on with our lives, making formula, sterilizing nipples, lugging diapers, bleaching burp cloths, stimulating the baby, pacifying him. There wasn't time for weeping.

CHAPTER

Two

Three years earlier . . .

Jeremy put the small glass bottle of warm urine in his inside suit pocket so it wouldn't get cold on the subway. It was a long morning. At eleven o'clock, I used the hall phone so my co-worker in the next cubicle couldn't hear me.

"It's positive," the nurse said. "Do you want to keep it?"

"What?"

"Do you want the baby?"

"Yes, well yes, of course."

At Saks on lunch hours, I fingered fine wool receiving blankets but didn't dare to buy. Waiting for the green light on Fifth Avenue, I thought, "I have life inside me; we will cross the street."

There had never been any doubt in my mind. The question was when, not if. There wasn't a lot of time to waste—Jeremy and I were both thirty when we married.

I miscarried on Labor Day. Eleven weeks.

"The baby would not have been healthy."

"It was God's will."

"Try again."

In the bathroom brushing my teeth, I'd remember I hadn't taken my temperature before getting out of bed. Shaking down the thermometer one morning, I dropped it and little balls of mercury scurried across the tile floor. The dips and plateaus of my basal temperature chart satisfied my gynecologist—I was ovulating.

"Try to have intercourse every other day between days ten and twenty after your period begins" were the doctor's orders. I'd put a pillow underneath my hips and remain in bed for an hour after making love, with my knees close to my chest. "Jeremy," I'd call out from the bedroom, "could you bring me the *Times*, please? I'm waiting for the sperm to make its way up."

After day twenty, the pressure was off. Anxiety mounted again after day thirty-five, a more passive activity—waiting. I remained hopeful month after month after month. But always blood, no baby.

My gynecologist recommended having a radiologist inject dye into my uterus, then take an X-ray. Anywhere the dye was absorbed would show up white on the black screen. I shuddered as the dye went through my body. The radiologist pointed out the left horn of the uterus and the dangling fallopian fingers. The right horn and tubes didn't appear on the screen. The radiologist suggested another injection of dye, this time into the kidneys, to see if perhaps my right kidney was missing. Apparently women missing a uterine horn are often missing the corresponding kidney. "Anybody that drinks wine like you do should have two kidneys," Jeremy said when I related the details of the process. I did have two kidneys.

A medical book in my company's library informed me that a unicornate uterus, though rare, does not prevent conception and successful pregnancy.

"What next?" I asked Dr. Doyle. He referred me to an endocrinologist to determine whether my problem was hormonal. This visit proved to be an all-day affair, consisting mostly of sitting back in a recliner chair. A vial of blood was taken from a vein in my arm. Then I drank glucose (my choice of lime, grape, or cherry) and sat in the recliner until I was ready to go to the bathroom and urinate into a paper cup. This glucose tolerance test was repeated several times over a five-hour period. The book I'd brought along to read was *Waiting for Cacciato*, a National Book Award winner about Vietnam. It was definitely the wrong choice. The sight of several strangers lolling in recliners in a windowless room, periodically trotting off to the bathroom with little paper cups, was depressing enough without reading about the horrors of war.

Six hours and $375 later, I was allowed to go home. The finding: My thyroid gland was slightly hypoactive; a Vitamin B complex pill swallowed daily should perk it up. The doctor's Mercedes was parked outside his office. Not a major expense for him, I figured.

Jeremy's semen was analyzed under a microscope; the sperm count and motility were normal. Both Jeremy and I visited Dr. Doyle so he could see that we wanted him to be more aggressive. He suggested a D&C, dilation and curettage, of the womb. The cervix is opened slightly with a hooked little instrument, then the uterus is scraped clean. A new beginning. Dr. Doyle also planned to do a laparoscopy, which entails inserting a long narrow tube with a mirror on the end through the navel. The mirror reflects the uterine cavity and tubes and ovaries. "If I find anything during the laparoscopy, I might go further," said Dr. Doyle.

When I woke and tried to sit up, I couldn't. There was a dull steady ache in my abdomen. I felt under my hospital gown and found a thick bandage over my stomach. I guess he found something, I thought. There was a needle taped to my hand and a bottle hung upside down next to the bed. A nurse came in and felt my forehead. "You are one hot hamburger," she said. "Maggie," said Dr. Doyle, standing behind the nurse, "you look beautiful." He kissed my forehead, forever gallant. "I found a tiny little right horn, smaller than my thumb. It had a good fallopian tube growing from it. So I took the horn out and I attached the fallopian tube to the left horn. I took a few fibroid tumors out, too. So now maybe you'll get pregnant."

Jeremy and I spent a week at some friends' cottage on Cape Cod just after the surgery. We enjoyed misty beach walks and rereading favorite books by the fireplace. Over the next few months, my periods were just late enough to get my hopes up. Then I'd have horrendous cramps and finally the inevitable bleeding.

One day a friend at work told me about an unmarried pregnant friend of hers who had given her baby up for adoption. I called her attorney and stammered and stuttered out my interest. The lawyer finally said, "What is it you want to know? If I know of other babies for adoption? I don't." I felt like an idiot.

I phoned the doctor who had delivered the baby. He was friendly and listened patiently as I poured out my history. "You know," he said when I had finished, "with that surgery and those fibroids, your chances of getting pregnant probably aren't all that good. And obviously you've been thinking about adoption. There seem to be lots of babies available from Latin American countries, like Chile or Brazil. Those kids are so cute with their brown skin; they look like Italians. Get some information from the Chilean or Brazilian consulates."

It was just what I needed. Somebody knowledgeable

and disinterested enough to say, "Look, A doesn't sound possible for you. Why not try B?" I wasn't offended or depressed. It was exciting to feel so directed. The consulates gave me the information and I wrote letters to various adoption centers in Latin America.

We made an appointment with the director of adoptions of the Children's Aid Society, where Jeremy had done architectural work. "There are no white infants," she said. "I can't even put you on a waiting list. Women are keeping their babies now. Or they're having them adopted privately."

Jeremy and I didn't feel we could handle a handicapped child or an older child. We wanted as close an approximation to a healthy newborn infant as possible.

An old friend, relocated from New York to California, visited us over the New Year holiday. I told her we were investigating adoption. She said, "Remember Eileen Conroy? She adopted a baby two years ago. The biological parents are Irish. The baby is beautiful. Eileen did a lot of research first, so I'm sure she'll have some leads for you."

I wrote Eileen without any particular hope and was surprised to receive a long-distance call from her a week or so later.

"Maggie?" She sounded very excited. "I may have some good news for you. I know a woman who is going to have a baby in June. She's twenty-eight years old and is from El Salvador. She works as a domestic for my neighbors and has no family here. She wants the baby to be adopted. She has asked me to help her find adoptive parents because of my daughter and because I speak Spanish. Would you be interested?"

"Eileen, how amazing! It's wonderful. Let me call my husband and call you right back."

Jeremy said, "Yes. Tell her yes."

"Just yes?" I said.

"Yes. Call her back and tell her yes."

"Eileen, we are interested."

"Oh, Maggie, I'm so glad. Angelina—that's her name—Angelina Rodriguez—is a lovely person. She's a very healthy young woman and she's had good prenatal care. What can I tell you about her? She's fair-skinned, with dark hair and brown eyes. She comes from a family of seven. Maggie, I can tell you from my daughter Kathleen that the bonding is there right from the beginning. Oh, I'm so excited."

"What should we do now?" I asked Eileen. I was excited, too, but nervous. Sitting in my office in the middle of corporate America, twenty-six stories up in the air and talking about having a baby in four months!

"Well," said Eileen, "I think you should write a letter to Angelina's employers, the Arnaldos, and tell them a little bit about you and Jeremy. Why you're interested in adoption, why you feel you'd be good parents, and so forth. What your lives are like, your families. And then we can see if Angelina is interested in you.

"Usually the adoptive parents assume the medical costs and some upkeep during pregnancy, but you can discuss all that later. You'll probably need three or four solid references from people who know you and Jeremy as a couple and as professionals—a clergyman, personal references. You know, 'I've known the Ryans for ten years and know they're seeking to adopt a baby . . . ' "

I hung up the phone and wandered down the hall to find an atlas. I wasn't even positive where El Salvador was. Squeezed in between Guatemala and Nicaragua, it didn't look far away at all.

That night, I wrote the letter:

January 3, 1982

Dear Mr. Arnaldo,

My husband and I are interested in adopting a baby, and

Eileen Conroy has directed us to you. Eileen and I met in New York when she was living here several years ago, and I've kept in contact with her through another shared friend who lives in Los Angeles and sees Eileen several times a year. I knew Eileen and Dan had adopted an infant, so I wrote to her for advice.

We are thrilled at the possibility of adopting a child from El Salvador. Letters to Colombian and Chilean adoption agencies have resulted in the receipt of complicated forms, which suggest time-consuming procedures with anonymous people. We are investigating these routes, but we are anxious to have a child as soon as possible.

A little background information on us as a couple and as professionals:

Jeremy is an architect and a partner in the firm Ryan and Schmidt. After graduation from college (University of Illinois, 1969, B.A., Architecture), he came to New York and worked for an architectural firm for four years. He then worked for the Urban Development Corporation for two years. Next, he went to Africa for a year, representing a New York-based Nigerian firm. He returned to New York and began his own firm in 1977. Ryan and Schmidt design and administer a variety of architectural projects—new and rehab apartment buildings in the Bronx, Queens, and Staten Island; restaurant design in New York City; rehab of the bird house in the Central Park Zoo; and much more. They have an office on Broadway and employ about eight people.

Jeremy's parents live in St. Louis. His father, recently retired, worked as an insurance agent. Jeremy has two brothers: Doug, an engineer, who lives with his wife and child in San Diego, California; and George, an accountant, who lives with his wife in San Jose, California. Jeremy's sister, Mary, is a medical illustrator currently finishing a two-year contract with Project Hope in Jamaica.

I have worked in publishing for several years. My resume (I keep it up-to-date as I do freelance editing) is enclosed.

I am the second youngest in a family of six children. My father (who died in 1974) was a doctor; my mother left her nursing job to become a homemaker when they married. I have two brothers and three sisters. Joe is married, has two adopted children, lives in Illinois, and is an athletic director and basketball coach. Katherine lives in Illinois, has taught first grade for several years, will complete her law studies and take the bar exam this summer. Ann is married, has two children, lives in Honolulu, and teaches nursing in a community college. Helen is married, has two children, lives in Miami, and works as a nurse. Alan lives in Illinois and works as a restaurant manager.

I was raised in Chicago, then moved to New York to seek a publishing career. Jeremy and I had met on a blind date in Chicago in 1968, but we didn't see each other again until we recognized each other in a vegetable store in New York City in 1974. After dating for several years, we were married in July of 1979.

Both of us wanted very much to have children right away when we married. I've been seeing a gynecologist who has done many fertility-type tests over the past two years. Both of us have seen an endocrinologist. While it's not absolutely certain that we cannot have our own biological children, we prefer not to wait any longer. If we adopt a child and have biological children, too, all the better.

We have a good income (Jeremy, about $40,000; me, about $25,000) and will be moving into our own loft on April 1. It has plenty of space (about 2000 square feet) for a child. Parks and good schools are nearby.

I always assumed I would have children and knew I would be a good mother. Marrying Jeremy made me feel doubly sure that we would be good and loving parents. I feel a lack in my life where children should be and I'm very anxious to share our love with a child.

I have asked my gynecologist, Dr. Stephen Doyle; Peter Schmidt, a professional and personal friend of Jeremy's; Frances Young, a colleague and friend of mine; and Fr. Dave Geier, an old friend of Jeremy's family, to write you with references. Dr. Doyle can attest to my good health, and

Jeremy's doctor can send a bill of health if you want it. I'm enclosing a picture taken of us this past weekend.

We eagerly await hearing from you. Please call (collect, of course) if that's easiest.

Sincerely yours,
Marguerite Ryan

In several days Eileen called to say that Angelina was pleased with the prospect of Jeremy and me adopting her child. She liked the fact that my brother had two adopted children. She also liked all the aunts, uncles, and cousins the baby would have.

"We'll have to get a lawyer," Jeremy said.

"Really?" I said. "Is that necessary?"

"Of course," he said. "I'll call Elizabeth and Bill and see if they know anyone in San Francisco." He called our California friends and they gave us three names. The first attorney Jeremy called said, "It's not possible. If the baby is born in California and you live in New York, an adoption is not possible." The second attorney's secretary said her boss was seriously ill and was not taking any new clients. The third attorney wouldn't take our call.

"This is ridiculous," I said to Jeremy, and dialed San Francisco information. I asked the operator to give me the first few numbers listed under "adoption." Five minutes later, I'd been told by a Sacramento agency that what we were embarking on was called an interstate adoption. The biological mother would initiate the process by filing an application in Sacramento. Sacramento would then forward this application to Albany for New York's approval.

We arranged a meeting with Saul Levine, a New York attorney who had handled personal affairs for Jeremy's partner. "Maybe you could just simplify everything by doing what another client of mine did a few years ago,"

Saul said. "Listen to this. This young girl, in Hong Kong, she's about twenty, gets pregnant. She knows her parents would flip out if she has an illegitimate kid. So she arranges to visit her aunt in New York for several months. When it's time for the baby to be born, she registers at the hospital in the aunt's name. When the kid is a few weeks old, the girl goes back to her family in Hong Kong, leaving the kid in New York with the aunt. OK. After a few years the aunt decides she wants to make things official. She comes to me to ask how she can adopt this kid. I say, 'Whose name is on the birth certificate as the mother?' She says, 'Mine.' I say, 'OK, legally you're the mother. What's to adopt? Case closed.' "

"What does this have to do with us?" I asked.

Saul said, "It's simple. You get Angelina to come to New York a month or so before the baby is due. She goes to a doctor and uses your name. In the hospital she's Maggie Ryan. When the baby is born, it's yours. No adoption necessary."

"Um, that sounds pretty weird," I said.

"Not to mention illegal," said Jeremy.

"Just for starters," I said, "what if she dies giving birth? Then I'd be dead."

"It was just an idea," said Saul.

"OK," said Jeremy, "let's figure out what we need to do. Do we need two attorneys, Saul? One in California, too?"

"I think so," Saul said. "If the kid is gonna be born there, you need a California attorney. I don't know California law."

On the way home I said to Jeremy, "Is he for real?"

Jeremy said, "He's a character, isn't he?"

"Do you think he can handle the adoption?"

"I don't see why not," said Jeremy. "It should be pretty straightforward."

One day in early April I received a phone call from a Neil Hernandez in San Francisco. He introduced himself as an attorney who rented office space from Philip Arnaldo, Angelina's employer. Apparently Mr. Arnaldo had suggested that Neil might handle the California legalities. Neil had already researched California adoption law and seemed to know what had to be done. We had a long conversation in which he enlightened me about the Interstate Compact. Fortunately Neil was bilingual and could communicate freely in Spanish with Angelina. He would help her fill out the application.

Neil said, "I really feel that Angelina is making a sensible decision on a rational level. For her, it's not just financial. The support is emotional and psychological. Her family is poor; her father is dead. She wants the child to have the best."

We gave Saul Levine's address and phone number to Neil so they could confer about who should do what when.

Toward the end of our conversation, Neil said, "And then there's the question of my fee. It's three thousand dollars."

"Who pays that?" I asked.

"Well, you do, of course," he laughed. "I'm representing you."

"Oh," I said. "I guess I thought we were sharing you with Angelina."

"A lawyer can only serve one client," he said. "And Angelina can't afford a lawyer. If you can send me fifteen hundred dollars right away," he continued, "I'd appreciate it. The other half should be paid when the adoption is finalized."

"Oh, well, OK," I said. Three thousand dollars sounded like a lot.

"You know, Maggie," Neil said, "I want this adoption

to be like a blue-chip corporate merger. I don't want her upsetting the apple cart five years down the road."

"Of course not," I responded. "We want it to be perfect, too. It sounds like you've done a lot of work already. We're pleased."

From April to June both Jeremy and I had several phone conversations with Neil. "He looks like Napoleon with darker skin," Neil reported after he met with the biological father to get his prebirth consent. "He's thirty years old, about five foot six, round head, high forehead, brown eyes, dark brown short hair, bit of a pot belly. He was a paratrooper ten years ago in the San Salvadoran–Honduran war. He lost the ends of four fingers in a grenade explosion."

Neil said, "My interpretation is that he's a randy fellow. He had a fling, she got pregnant. I think he's relieved to be off the hook. He's a nice fellow, not an ogre. His married sister probably said, 'You'll be a father. Make appropriate noises.' But Antonio isn't interested in custody. He signed the consent willingly."

"Good," I said. "Has everything that can be done now been done?"

"Yes," said Neil. "What I'd like would be for all four of you—Angelina, Antonio, Jeremy, and you—to go into court when Angelina and Antonio sign the postbirth consents here in San Francisco."

"All four of us?" I said, alarmed. It sounded far too cozy.

"Why not?" asked Neil.

"I guess I thought we'd remain more anonymous," I said.

"Maggie, I want this adoption to be as secure as possible legally," said Neil.

"All right," I said. "I'm sure you know what you're doing."

My concern could now focus solely on the pregnancy and delivery. I called the pediatrician recommended by my gynecologist. "You'll want to get the APGAR scores—how soon the baby cries after delivery, how blue the skin is, and so forth—the blood type. Try to get as much information as possible about the biological mother and father—any family history of diabetes, cancer, and so forth."

I asked my sisters, mothers of sons, their feelings on circumcision. Positive. "He'll look like the other kids in the locker room." And "If it has to be done for some reason when he's four or five, it would be extremely painful and threatening psychologically."

Eileen was to call us when Angelina went to the hospital. We were on hold.

CHAPTER

Three

When June turned into July, my nerves started to fray. I jumped every time the phone rang. "We're still waiting," we'd say to my sisters or Jeremy's mother. "We'll let you know when we know."

Angelina went into labor on July 16. My boss was on the phone when I looked into his office, so I held my elbows in my hands and rocked my arms back and forth. Then I flapped my arms up and down and waved good-bye. He grinned. He had been forewarned.

It was 90 degrees in New York, and my cotton sundress stuck to my back in the cab to LaGuardia. I'd waited so long for this moment, but all I felt was sweaty and anxious that we'd miss our plane. The taxi crawled along in a mire of traffic. Jeremy was backseat driving.

Just before boarding, Jeremy called Neil, our California lawyer, who said, "It's a boy and he's big." A son. Christopher. Christopher Monahan Ryan. It sounded right.

The movie was *Rocky II*. Mrs. Rocky gave birth to a boy with an enormous amount of black hair. I sipped champagne and mused about Christopher's hair. Jeremy studied a map of San Francisco. I felt like telling someone but I didn't. ("I just had a baby"?)

We rented a car at the airport and finally found San Francisco General Hospital. The lobby was deserted, not even an information desk. Finally we found a wall directory and learned that the nursery was on the fifth floor.

"We're the adoptive parents of the baby born to Ms. Rodriguez," we told the nurse at the fifth floor desk.

"She's right down this hall," pointed the nurse.

"No," I said, "we want to see the baby."

"Oh, I see," she said. "Well, the nursery is down that hall."

A chubby red-haired nurse beamed at us. "We've been waiting for you. I told him you were coming from New York as fast as you could." She gave us white gowns and continued, "He's the biggest baby in the nursery—eight pounds, fifteen ounces." Her bubbling eased my nervousness. I looked at the nine or ten tiny babies in their identical white boxes. Which one was Christopher? I felt I should recognize him. The nurse wheeled over a cart holding a wide-awake baby with a headful of black hair and a bloody bruise in the corner of his left eye.

"Here he is," she announced proudly.

"Oh," was all that I could manage. I wasn't sure what to think. He looked funny. His hair was all slicked down with a part, but it stood up in a coxcomb at the crown. He was swaddled so tightly in a blanket that it was impossible to see anything but his head. I wondered fleetingly if he had arms and legs.

"Would you like to see all of him?" the nurse asked, laughing.

She unwrapped the shroudlike receiving blanket layer by layer and there he was—a stick-legged little creature with wrinkled fingers. His full head of hair made him look much older than eight hours. Imagine anyone being eight hours old. With the three-hour time difference between East and West coasts, we'd managed to leave New York just after Christopher was born, fly 3,000 miles, rent a car, find an out-of-the-way hospital, and still miss only eight hours of our son's life.

"You'd probably like to get acquainted with him alone," said the nurse. "This little room has a rocking chair. I'll get you a bottle and you can feed him. Dr. Lindstrom, who delivered him, wanted to know when you arrived, so I'll call him."

Jeremy rocked Christopher while I hovered jealously. "Don't you think I should give him the bottle?" I said.

"Why?" said Jeremy, smiling and handing me the baby.

"Because," I announced, "I am the mother."

"Congratulations, mom," Jeremy said. "Hold the bottle a little higher; he's getting air."

A very young man in hospital greens stood at the door. "Hi, I'm Dr. Lindstrom. Congratulations."

Jeremy gave him a cigar.

"It was a difficult delivery," said the doctor. "He just wasn't coming out. Ms. Rodriguez was really strong during the labor; she did a great job. Anyway, he just wasn't coming out. We didn't want to do a Caesarean, so I delivered him with forceps, pulled him out."

"Is that how his eye got bruised?" asked Jeremy.

"Yes. The forceps pinched that skin a little. But the eye socket prevented any real damage. I had our plastic surgeon look at it and he didn't think surgery would be necessary."

(Plastic surgery on a baby! I thought wildly.)

"I think it will be all right," said Jeremy. "Maybe a little scar."

I marveled at the baby's long fingernails.

"I think he cooked a little too long," said Dr. Lindstrom.

"He was supposed to be born June 15, a month ago," I said. "Is it possible to be that late?"

"Well, maybe Ms. Rodriguez got the dates mixed up," he said. "My daughter had really long nails when she was born. I was afraid to use scissors on her, so I bit them off. You might try that."

Dr. Lindstrom said Christopher had bilirubin—his skin was jaundiced, yellow. Jeremy's response: "I thought Billy Reuben was a New York sandwich." The doctor said the bilirubin would recede when Christopher's liver "kicked in."

We talked a little about New York, often a place of fascination for Californians. It seemed so natural and comfortable to be sitting there at one o'clock in the morning, rocking our baby and chatting with the doctor who had delivered him.

At the end of her shift, the friendly nurse came in to say good-night. She asked if we wanted a cap for Christopher. She'd put them on all the other babies, she told us. The surgical gauze stretch bandage fit Christopher's head snugly; the end was secured with tape. He now bore a strong resemblance to Yoda of *Star Wars*. "Keeps the body heat in," the nurse assured us. Christopher seemed to be in good hands at San Francisco General. Now it was time to put ourselves to bed; it was four in the morning New York time.

We felt grimy and exhausted as we drove into the elegant courtyard of the Stanford Court on Nob Hill. This treat had been reserved by a friend in New York whose brother was the hotel's manager. The room was gorgeous—silk draperies, plush carpeting, a mahogany armoire discreetly housing a television. The manager had thoughtfully left us fresh flowers and a huge basket filled with splits of champagne, fresh fruit, and biscuits, and a note—"Congratulations!"

"I think I like this baby business," I said to Jeremy as we munched and sipped in bed.

Early the next morning, we called our far-flung relatives (from the bathroom phone). We limited room service to coffee, fearing an astronomical charge if we dared include orange juice or croissants. I wore the linen jacket I'd suggested Jeremy buy me for Mother's Day.

We checked out of the hotel and rushed off to the hospital. Christopher was alert and hungry. A nurse told us that he probably saw more of me than other newborns saw their mothers because I was not bedridden or drowsy.

We sat rocking and feeding Christopher while various hospital staff came by. Dr. Faye Hill, the pediatrician, was young (no one at San Francisco General seemed to be over thirty) and direct. She said we could probably take Christopher from the hospital the next evening.

We took lots of photographs that day. My favorite: Jeremy holding Christopher against his shoulder. All that shows of Jeremy is a little swatch of reddish beard and the lapel of his blue suit sticking out from under the surgical gown. Chris is peering over Jeremy's shoulder and looks like a little chipmunk—wrapped in the everpresent receiving blanket—adorable and dependent.

I felt totally comfortable with Christopher, felt he belonged to me and I to him, from that first night. He filled me up. I didn't have much left for Angelina. But every little while Angelina would flash into my thoughts. She couldn't be very far away from us—down this or that corridor. What was she doing? Sleeping? Crying? Was she at peace with herself? Did she yearn to see Christopher? Would her breasts drip milk?

The hospital social worker had been in touch with Angelina since May. Pat Henderson had apprised Angelina of the various alternatives open to her—a foster home if she decided on temporary care for the baby, food programs that might be available to an illegal alien, and so on. It was the social worker's job to help Angelina reach her own decision about the baby, and to be aware that there were options if she changed her mind about the adoption.

Pat said that Angelina wanted to meet Jeremy and me. I was apprehensive. What would we say? She didn't speak English; we didn't speak Spanish.

Overnight, I thought more about a meeting. We would meet Angelina. We had Christopher. She had the right to see our happiness. We would say thank you; he is beautiful.

I suggested to Neil that Father Ramo, a Spanish-speaking priest in whom Angelina had confided, be present at the meeting. He could interpret and buffer as well: "OK, Angelina has to rest now; I think the Ryans should say good-bye." He could stay on awhile to comfort her, to reassure her that she'd made the right decision.

But by the next morning, Angelina had decided it would be too emotional to meet us. I was relieved. We gave the social worker a bouquet of roses for Angelina. She gave us a bag of shower gifts that Angelina had received.

Christopher was circumcised that morning while Jeremy and I watched. The doctor crossed his own legs as he stood over the baby. "I just can't help it," he said. "I do this every time." We laughed at his physical manifestation of empathy for a fellow male but we winced for Christopher. His body lay in a Styrofoam circle with Velcro strips securing his wrists and ankles. He wailed loudly as the doctor snipped. A few minutes later he fell fast asleep. The pediatrician said we could take him from the hospital as soon as he urinated, a sign that the circumcision was successful, probably early that evening.

Neil Hernandez stared at me as we shook hands. "It's amazing," he said, "how much you and Angelina look alike."

"Really," I said, "that's good. So Christopher will look like me."

I was rather surprised myself by Neil's appearance. He was dressed in jeans and a plaid flannel shirt, hardly typical attorney attire. His smooth, rich voice had led me to believe we'd be meeting a tall, distinguished man in a three-piece suit. But Neil was short, with a slight build, and very boyish looking.

"Everything seems to be in order," he said. "Angelina signed the placement-for-adoption form yesterday after the social worker translated it. I had hoped to go into court for a final consent before the domestic relations judge went on vacation, but the birth was later than we expected. So we'll just wait for August to go to court."

"We'll be taking Christopher from the hospital tonight," Jeremy said.

"When will Angelina go home?" I asked Neil.

"Probably tomorrow," he said.

"Where will she go? Back to Carmine Street?" I asked. Angelina spent her weekends in San Francisco, where she rented a room in a boarding house.

"I guess so," he said.

"And then will she go back to work for the Arnaldos?" I was concerned that Angelina have a support system to stave off the postpartum blues.

"She can use the hospital's social services," said Neil. "She can have follow-up appointments with the social worker if she wants them."

"When you see Angelina again, please tell her how happy we are," I said.

"Of course," said Neil. "Christopher looks good in your arms. The three of you make a nice family."

I'd forgotten how cool San Francisco can be in summer. We stopped at a children's boutique and bought a warm yellow blanket to wrap Christopher up in for his first trip outdoors. He left the hospital wearing the surgical gauze hat again. The hospital staff gave us a large supply of diapers and formula, enough to last until we got home to New York.

Now we would have Christopher all to ourselves. Nonetheless, we felt sad to leave the cocoon of the hospital and its warm staff. Jeremy took a picture of Christopher and me in the parking lot just before we got into the car. Chris's big eyes narrowed into slits from his first exposure to the sun. I held him tightly on my lap as we drove to our friends' house in nearby Belmont. He was so still. My arms ached from holding him so stiffly; I had to concentrate to relax. Jeremy's glance flickered back and forth from Christopher to the road. It seemed fairy-taleish to be driving along a California freeway with my husband and our new baby.

Our friends' two little daughters hovered around Christopher like miniature nannies. Every few minutes they'd run back to their bedroom, then emerge with another item of doll clothing to donate to Chris's minimal layette.

Jeremy's brother and his wife drove over from Saratoga to join us for dinner. Christopher provided an instant bridge between friends and family. After dinner, Jeremy's brother took us to his home for the weekend.

Spending the weekend with my sister-in-law in Saratoga turned out to be an excellent idea for more than purely family reasons. Lisa had three sons and lots of good advice for a new mother. She had bought a wicker bassinet and sewed a dust ruffle, liner, and pillow cases for it. The legs on the bassinet were collapsible, so we could take it on the plane. She helped me give Christopher his first bath and shampoo. She suggested a sunbath to expedite drying up the umbilical cord. She worried about cold feet and rushed out to buy booties. She taught me how to burp him midway through a bottle. She warmed his formula in the microwave. It was like having a private nursemaid.

I was afraid to fall asleep the first night. Convinced I wouldn't hear Christopher when he awoke, I lay in bed awake, with the bassinet by my side, until almost 3:00 A.M., and had just drifted off when he cried. Jeremy and I jumped up together.

When we returned to New York, we "received." UPS brought gifts every day for two weeks. My sister and her husband drove up from Miami with their two young sons. Christopher was baptized at home when he was twelve days old. My sister and brother-in-law were god-parents.

My sister introduced Christopher to pacifiers, despite the pediatrician's objections. "Sucking is comfort," she stated firmly. Christopher seemed to agree. The pacifier got him through the third act of *Peter Pan.* We all went roller skating in Central Park. I changed Chris's diapers in the Federalist Courtyard of the Metropolitan Museum's American Wing.

Jeremy often came home from work for lunch with Chris and me. He was gentle with Christopher, allowing a new softness to bloom. Humming "Edelweiss," he'd sit back in the big mahogany rocker and Chris would fall asleep in his arms. Then Jeremy, tall and broad-shouldered, would slowly bend to lower Christopher into his crib.

We spent much of August and early September traveling with Christopher to our families and friends—the Long Island Sound, the Catskill Mountains, my family in Illinois, Jeremy's family in St. Louis. Everyone loved the beautiful baby with all that hair and those big black eyes. He elicited so many memories of my babyhood, or Jeremy's, or another sibling's, from my mother and Jeremy's mother. We did very little other than sit around talking, watching Chris.

Back in the city in September, we started to get into more of a routine. I enjoyed strolling around Soho and the Village with Christopher in the Snugli. Even strangers gave us a warm response. Venturing into the playground in Washington Square was exhilarating, not because Christopher could do much yet, but because I could meet other mothers and share Dr. Spockisms.

The lunch with Saul Levine shattered our idyllic autumn. After talking with Eileen Conroy, I called our California lawyer, Neil Hernandez.

"Neil, it's Maggie Ryan. Is it true what Levine said?"

"Maggie, I'm so sorry. Angelina went to a Legal Aid kind of place and found herself a new lawyer. Miguel Posito. He called me yesterday and said she's withholding her consent."

"But why?"

"Well, you know . . ." Neil's voice trailed off.

"You know what?"

"She first called me in August," he said.

"And?"

"She said she felt bad. I told her to call Mike Cole," he said, referring to the *pro bono* lawyer whom he had found for Angelina through his parish priest.

"Neil, you never mentioned that call to us," I said.

"I never heard from her after that, so I figured she

stuck to her original decision," Neil said. "I didn't want to scare you and Jeremy without cause."

"All you told us was that she would go to court in October."

"That's what I thought, too," he said. "Mike Cole thought so. Then I get a call from this Posito person saying that Cole withdrew from the situation when Angelina decided to withhold her consent. Cole is not willing to represent her now that she's changed her mind."

"Neil, Jeremy and I spent all summer with Christopher without a care in the world. And now this bomb drops on us. What are we going to do?"

Silence from Neil. I couldn't even conjure up a picture of Angelina, because I'd never met her. She was supposedly pretty, with rosy cheeks, dark hair, and brown eyes. "I wish I could talk to her," I said.

"Maybe that would be helpful," Neil replied.

"Well, maybe you can talk to her," I said. "She always called you instead of Mike Cole, anyway. I think it helps, your speaking Spanish. And she told you you reminded her of Father Ramo. Remember? When she said some people said she had a black heart to think of adoption for her baby, you said only God knows what kind of heart she has."

"Maggie, I'm *your* lawyer. She has her own lawyer, whether it's Cole before or Posito now. I'm supposed to talk to her lawyer, not to her. That's the reason I went to my church and asked for a recommendation for *pro bono* counsel, remember? So there wouldn't be this conflict of interest."

"Oh, yeah," I said. My crash course in adoption law had left me almost as naive as before. I told Neil that Jeremy and I planned to see a New York adoption lawyer—someone with experience—for advice.

Norman Bernstein was recommended to Jeremy by a

client who has two adopted daughters. We met Norman in his office two days after the lunch with Levine. Norman had encountered this change-of-mind situation before and said that from his experience our best hope was that Angelina might just give up. We would wear her down. That, he claimed, was what happened often. He suggested that I write to Angelina and appeal to her emotionally by giving her an idea of what kind of family life Christopher has with us.

"Of course, I can't promise you anything," said Norman. "If you take this to court, it'll buy you time. If you lose, it will be that much harder to give him up when he's older."

CHAPTER
Four

October 7, 1982

Dear Fr. Ramo,

I'm writing today so that this letter will be in your hands when you return from Guatemala on October 13.

My husband, Jeremy, and I are the adoptive parents of the child born to Angelina Rodriguez on July 16. We talked to you a few days after the baby was born.

Miss Rodriguez's willing surrender of the child was thought by all of us to be the best possible decision, albeit a difficult one. However, our view of the situation is now clouded since Miss Rodriguez apparently may be changing her mind about the adoption. She has spoken to a new lawyer at Legal Aid and has told him she wants the baby back.

The child is now twelve weeks old. We love him very much; he is an integral part of our lives and our home.

Obviously, we're very upset and concerned and feel strongly that Miss Rodriguez needs good counsel. Her earlier decisions focused on the child's best interests. Now she is focusing on her own situation. Naturally, she must be feeling some loneliness and sadness, but we think it is a mistake to try to solve that loneliness with the child. Her attitude should be balanced by her hopes and opportunities for the child as he grows up with us.

Childrearing is an important and difficult task; all the necessary support (economic, family, psychological, social) may not be available to Miss Rodriguez. She and her new lawyer met with our lawyer (Neil Hernandez) yesterday. There is no definite action as a result of that meeting; we're all in a kind of limbo.

During this interim period, we are hopeful that counseling can be made available to Miss Rodriguez. The prebirth counseling that she had was not carried into the postbirth time.

You were an important part of that counseling, and we're appealing to you to speak with Miss Rodriguez as soon as possible. Ultimately, we believe that we should meet with her. Time is clearly becoming an important factor. If Miss Rodriguez could meet with me she would hopefully recognize my mother-to-mother appeal; now we seem to be just "the couple from New York."

Our baby is happy and healthy in our home. We are not willing to consider a simple surrender. The disruption in our child's life if he has to be taken from his home will be enormous (see attached excerpts from studies on this point).

Please call us collect so we can discuss the situation.

Thank you, Fr. Ramo.

Sincerely,
Marguerite Monahan Ryan

cc: Neil Hernandez

October 24, 1982

Miguel M. Posito
442 Alabon Street
San Francisco, California 94111

Dear Mr. Posito:
This will acknowledge receipt of your letter of October

16, 1982, which has been forwarded to the Ryans' New York attorney, Mr. Norman Bernstein.

I am informed that Mr. Bernstein has filed a petition for adoption in the Ryans' behalf in the Family Court of the State of New York, County of New York, under Docket No. Misc. 583.

Per our telephone conversation of last Wednesday, I am withdrawing from further involvement in the case, and you are hereby advised that I no longer represent Mr. and Mrs. Jeremy and Marguerite Ryan. Henceforth you should communicate directly with:

Mr. Norman Bernstein
160 West 37th Street, Suite 326
New York, NY 10019
Telephone: (212) 223-6707

Very truly yours,
Neil D. Hernandez

cc: Mr. Norman Bernstein
Mr. and Mrs. Jeremy Ryan

November 5, 1982

Mr. Norman Bernstein
160 West 37th Street
Suite 326
New York, NY 10019

Re: Adoption of Lorenzo Rodriguez

Dear Mr. Bernstein:

I am representing Ms. Angelina Rodriguez, whose child is presently under the physical custody of your clients, the Ryans.

As you are probably aware, my client would like the Ryans to immediately return the child to her. It is my hope that this can be accomplished without protracted legal entanglements, as Ms. Rodriguez has not presented to the

New York Family Court a duly executed and acknowledged consent to the adoption.

Ms. Rodriguez, of course, is prepared to assume the cost of transporting the child back to San Francisco, or she can travel there to New York personally. As such, I would like to make appropriate arrangements as soon as possible.

If the Ryans refuse to comply with this request, I am prepared to file a petition for a Writ of Habeas Corpus pursuant to our penal code.

I would appreciate your responding as soon as possible. I may be contacted at (415) 951-6172 in the mornings (our time) and at the above number in the afternoon.

Respectfully,
Miguel M. Posito

cc: Angelina Rodriguez

November 15, 1982

Miss Angelina Rodriguez
117 Carmine Street
San Francisco, California 94112

Dear Angelina,

The last time I wrote you was ten months ago, in February. In that letter I told you how much my husband and I wanted to be parents. We had been waiting so long to have a baby! Apparently you liked what the letter said about us because you chose us.

We liked what we heard about you, and one important thing was that you seemed to be thinking of the baby so much. You wanted to do what was best for him. You wanted him to grow up in the home of a married couple, a mother and a father. You were so happy to hear about all the brothers and sisters of both my husband and me, and all the nieces and nephews. "How good for a child to grow up like that," you said. "I want what will be best for him." You wanted the luxury of a private adoption, the luxury of your own choice, your own decision.

Angelina, all your hopes and dreams came true. The baby was baptized Christopher Monahan Ryan in our home by our priest on July 27. The priest said, "There is so much love in this house today. Christopher is right where he belongs." My sister and her husband and two children came up from Florida to be godparents for Chris. They gave him a sterling silver cup engraved with CHRISTOPHER, JULY 16, 1982, 8 POUNDS, 15 OUNCES, 22 INCHES. Hands on a clock point to his time of birth—11:58 A.M.

In addition to the priest and family, several close friends were present to share our joy and witness our new son's baptism. We had champagne and a big dinner and even set off fireworks. It was a wonderful evening, one to remember forever. Christopher wore the silk christening gown that my husband and all his brothers and sister wore at their baptisms over the past forty years.

So many friends visited and brought gifts for Chris! He has twenty-five stuffed animals and drawers full of beautiful clothes. One friend embroidered T-shirts for Chris. One T-shirt has an apple on it, for New York, the "Big Apple," Christopher's home.

We went to Illinois so that Christopher could visit his grandmother, aunts, uncles, and cousins. My sister and her children were there from Hawaii. There were lots of parties; everybody was so happy for Jeremy and me and so excited about Christopher. My brother and his family live near a lake, so we swam a lot. Next summer we're renting a cottage on the shore; I'll teach Chris to swim.

Then we flew to St. Louis to introduce Chris to Jeremy's family. His parents were absolutely thrilled; they gave us a beautiful wooden crib bed as a gift. Jeremy's brother has a nine-month-old baby, Patrick, and Christopher had a wonderful time with his new cousin.

We've been at home for several months. We're building a new room for Christopher; it's almost finished and will be beautiful. I spend all my time with Christopher. I have worked carefully to arrange my schedule so that he eats, sleeps, plays, and goes for walks outdoors just the right amount of time to make him healthy and happy. When we go outside, I carry him in a baby pouch on my chest; he loves it! He is very attached to his mama, as I am to him. I will do whatever I can for him. I think it's very important for a little baby to have his mother at home, so I quit my job and don't plan to go back. Christopher needs me.

I love to watch Chris with my husband—they have such a good time together. Jeremy gets up during the night with Chris, feeds him, changes his diapers, takes him out for walks—everything. I couldn't possibly imagine trying to raise a child alone; sometimes I'm so tired at the end of the day. It's wonderful to know that Jeremy will come home every night and help me with Chris. Sometimes he comes home for lunch, too, as his office is only a few blocks from our home. I remember the first day we gave Chris a bath and shampoo all on our own; we were nervous at first, but now we're so experienced!

Angelina, it must be clear to you that we deeply love Christopher and are absolutely committed to him. You made the right decision when you chose us to be his parents. We want what you want—what is best for him. That is living and growing up with us here in New York.

You are a young woman, and we've been told that you're pretty and bright. Look to the future. Get on with your life. You made a decision that was final. I think we both know it is morally wrong for you to even think about changing your mind. Wrong to bring heartbreak into three innocent, trusting lives, wrong to deprive Christopher of what is best for him.

I offered to fly out to California to talk with you and you refused. The offer is still open. We will send you an airline ticket to New York if you prefer to talk here. We are willing to go through whatever we must go through to keep our son with us.

God be with you, Angelina.

> Very sincerely yours,
> Marguerite Monahan Ryan

November 18, 1982

Mr. Norman Bernstein
160 West 37th Street, Suite 326
New York, NY 10019

Re: Adoption of Lorenzo Rodriguez

Dear Mr. Bernstein:
I have been informed by my client that Mrs. Ryan
recently wrote a lengthy letter to her in an attempt to
discourage her from withholding consent for the adoption
of Lorenzo. As a result of this communication, my client
became extremely upset, which has adversely affected her
emotional and psychological well-being. In order to prevent
similar occurrences, please kindly advise your client to
refrain from such communications. If your client desires to
communicate anything to my client, I think that it would be
best for her to do so through you.

> Respectfully,
> Miguel M. Posito

cc: Angelina Rodriguez

Christmas card, December 1982:

We are grateful to you, Angelina. We love Christopher
deeply and he is so happy with us.

> Merry Christmas,
> Maggie, Jeremy, and Christopher Ryan

February 12, 1983

Dear Miss Maggie:
It is a pleasure for me to greet you. I wish that you be
well together with your husband and my son.
My reason for writing this letter to you is because I want
to know how is my son; I am very worried about him. I
would like to ask you a great favor of sending me some

photos of his baptism and another recent photo. I will be most thankful. And please tell me how is he, has he been ill, is he healthy. I have been thinking that since today it is very cold he could get sick.

OK. Take good care of yourself.

A kiss for my child.

Angelina Rodriguez

CHAPTER

Five

I responded to Angelina promptly, assuring her that Christopher was warm, perfectly healthy, and enjoying a well-balanced diet. I enclosed a photograph of Chris taken at his baptism, where he wore the silk coat Jeremy wore at his own baptism.

In April and again in May, I sent Angelina brief notes asking her to let us know her plans for the future. We were in limbo, I wrote, until we heard from her. She didn't answer me.

We were served papers just before Chris's first birthday. My in-laws were visiting from St. Louis. It was their fortieth wedding anniversary, and Chris and I were having lunch with them before they went off to a Broadway matinee. Jeremy was in Boston on business for the day.

I answered the buzzer. "I have some papers for you," a Spanish-sounding voice said. I froze and said nothing. I went back to the dining table. My father-in-law said, "What was that all about?"

"Oh, uh, Con Ed," I said. "It was Con Edison. Something about the gas meter in the basement. Let them buzz another floor. I can't go down to the basement now."

He buzzed again. "It's about the baby. You have to take these papers about the baby. You have to go to court."

"Call my lawyer," I said. "Don't buzz me again."

"You'd better get going," I said to my in-laws. "You don't want to be late."

I called Norman Bernstein. He said, "If he comes back, take the papers. We've got our own papers to file." Norman planned to file for adoption on the grounds that Angelina had abandoned Christopher.

Everyone became a potential process server. Men in the street. Women in the vegetable market around the block. If anyone walked close to Christopher and me, my heart started pounding faster. My sister Katherine, an attorney, told me that process servers go to great lengths to accomplish their missions. For example, she said, a persistent process server ran through the corridor of the intended's office building yelling "Fire, fire." He got his man on the fire stairs.

Christopher and I were enrolled in "Water Babies," a swimming class held three times weekly at Marymount College. Babies and mothers paddled around together in the skylight pool. Sometimes fathers and grandparents came to share the fun from poolside. Halfway through class one day, a young man in a business suit stalked into the pool area. He scrutinized the water carefully as if he had to identify everybody in it. "This is it," I thought. I couldn't very well dive underwater holding eleven-month-old Christopher. Suddenly, the man left. I guess his wife and baby weren't in class that day. I was trembling.

It wasn't so much that I was trying to avoid being served. It was more the anxiety of wondering when he or she would strike. We could always hope this would all go away. But somehow we knew it wouldn't. So why prolong our anxiety?

It wasn't until ten days later that the process server buzzed again. It was about nine o'clock at night. Jeremy went downstairs to meet him. A young Hispanic guy with curly hair and a pink baseball cap.

When Jeremy came back upstairs, he handed me a paper and said, "She's here."

"Who's here?"

"She's here, in New York," he said. "Look what it says under 'address.' "

Mill Street. Bronx. "You mean Angelina is in the Bronx?"

"That's what the form says. It lists her address as the Bronx."

"But how can that be? Who is she living with?" Of course Jeremy knew no more than I knew. The paper also said we were to appear in court in two weeks.

I became really paranoid. I imagined Angelina was camping on our doorstep. I couldn't believe she wouldn't come right over if she was in New York.

We went to Family Court with Norman Bernstein two weeks later.

Angelina wasn't at all what I had expected. She looked feisty, wearing tight jeans, a striped T-shirt, her hair all pulled to one side of her head in a long braid. The curly haired fellow with the pink baseball cap was with her and her lawyer.

Norman suggested that we talk informally with Angelina and her lawyer before appearing before a judge. I guess he hoped for an out-of-court settlement. We all sat around a small conference table in a small, windowless room. Jorge Cabas, the pink hat, came too; he was to serve as interpreter for Angelina.

Introductions were made. Angelina's lawyer was Nat Schwartz, a handsome, aggressive-looking man in his mid-fifties. He and Norman were extremely cordial to one another, laughing and joking.

"Maggie, is there something you would like to say to Angelina?" asked Norman.

My voice quavered as if I were addressing a large group. "What do you think a mother is?" I asked Angelina.

"A mother is someone who has a baby," answered Angelina through Jorge.

"And I have had a baby for a whole year," I said. "I became a mother by changing his diapers and getting up with him in the middle of the night and rocking him when he was crying and . . ." Norman's knee pressed against my thigh under the table. Oh oh. I was being too heavy-handed, too holier-than-thou.

Jorge said, "Angelina understands. But she wants her son."

A court clerk rapped on the door. "The judge is ready for you."

"OK," said Norman to Schwartz, "we gave it a shot."

We filed into the courtroom. Judge Miller said our case should be decided as quickly as possible because it involved an infant. He assigned Judge Millicent Finberg to our case and said we were to appear in front of her in three weeks. We all filed out.

"What happened?" I said to Jeremy. "Did I miss something?"

"No," he replied, "nothing happened. We're coming back in three weeks. This was just a preliminary to assign a judge to us."

"Well?" we said to Norman.

"I've never heard of Finberg, but I'll ask around," he said.

Jeremy, Christopher, and I went back to our rented cottage on Long Island's North Shore. We were completely secluded, high on a woodsy hill above the beach, several hundred yards from the road, surrounded by raspberry and rose bushes.

Christopher loved the water. He scrambled over the pebbled beach, splashed in the shore waves, pounced on minnows, pursed his lips at the taste of salt water. He took three-hour naps every afternoon and gobbled down broiled fish every night.

The friends we shared the cottage with had a small son, too. Alex and Christopher sat on the porch floor gnawing their corn on the cob, pictures of total contentment. I couldn't bring myself to tell Ed and Barbara about the "situation," as I'd come to call it. I'm not sure why.

My sister Katherine proposed a family reunion for a week in August. Since the points of origin for various siblings were Illinois, New York, and Miami (the trip was out of the question for my sister in Hawaii), we decided that an in-between spot should be chosen: Ocean Isle, North Carolina, a long strip of beach hanging off the outer banks into the Atlantic. There were five couples, five kids—including Christopher—and my mother, nestled into the big beach house. All fifteen of us participated in Chris's first steps. We'd sit on the deck chorusing, "One, two, three, four . . . sixteen, seventeen," and Chris would totter toward outstretched arms. We'd all clap and cheer. Each day resulted in several more steps. By the end of the week he was a full-fledged walker at twelve months.

My older brother and I watched the stars from the deck one night.

"What are you going to do?" he asked.

"You mean if we lose?" I said.

"Yes."

"I don't know."

"Would you consider anything radical?"

"Such as?"

"Well," he said, "I go to this baseball camp every summer. Another coach there is divorced and has two kids. His wife had custody of the kids and she moved to another state. The guy had the kids for two weeks earlier this summer. During the time the wife was mysteriously killed."

"Do you think he did it?" I asked Joe.

"He sure as hell had a motive," he said.

"Did anyone at the camp ask him about it?" I said.

"No."

"He'll be investigated," I said.

"I'm sure," said Joe.

"Well, I wouldn't be too sad if Angelina met with a sudden demise." I smiled thinly.

Joe looked at me closely. "Would you try something?"

"Joe, how could we? I'm not really concerned about the morality or immorality of all this. What Angelina has done is immoral. I'm more concerned about getting away with it. I mean, who would the first suspects be?"

"You're right," he said.

"And it's not as if we hang around with Mafia types. I imagine it's very difficult to have someone killed."

"Probably more expensive than difficult," he said.

"True. Where would we ever begin to check this out?"

"I don't know. Ask Alan?"

We laughed. My younger brother, Alan, has a network of friends in rather dubious places. "That's an idea," I said. "I mean, if I heard that Angelina had been run over by a bus on Park Avenue, I would be delighted. But hiring someone to do her in? I don't think I could really do that. Plus, imagine the fear of blackmail for the rest of our lives."

The stars were so bright. The breeze so gentle. Laughter from the bridge game inside trickled out onto the deck. Warmth. Security. Family.

The next morning, the kids were sculpting a sand turtle on the beach. Alan's girlfriend, Karen, was helping Christopher fly a kite. Alan and I stood kicking foam at the water's edge.

"Do you know anybody that could get us a birth certificate for Christopher?" I asked.

"He doesn't have one?"

"He has one, but it says 'Lorenzo Rodriguez.' We want one that says 'Christopher Ryan.' "

"Why, are you planning to split or something?"

"Maybe," I said. "We'd like to have the option to leave the country suddenly if we have to."

"I think I could get one for you," he said. "My friend Mike could probably do it."

"How much would it cost?"

"Probably a hundred."

"Great," I said. "Will you ask him right away?"

Later that day, as we peeled shrimp together, my sister Katherine said, "I hope you and Jeremy aren't thinking of running away with Christopher."

"Why not?" I said.

"Because it's dumb," she said. "What kind of life would you have, always hiding? How could you stay away from all of us?"

"I don't know," I said. "Jeremy thinks we could go to Europe. He could get a job someplace."

"He doesn't have any languages," Katherine said.

"Well, I have French."

"And what jobs did you have in Paris—salesclerk in a bookstore, au pair? Not great jobs for a family of three. And what about Christopher? You'd never be able to let him out of your sight. He might not come home from school one day."

"It would be difficult," I said.

"It would be insane," Katherine said. "What about us, your family? What about Christmas, holidays?"

"Katherine, I don't know what we're going to do."

"Promise me you won't do anything without telling me first."

"I promise."

My sister Helen washed the dishes and I dried. "Have you thought at all about running away with Christopher?" she said.

I sighed. Maybe we should call a family conference and answer everyone's questions at the same time.

"We have thought about it, yes. I don't know what we're going to do."

"Don't do it. Look at Abby Hoffman. He just came up from being underground for seven years and said it was terrible. Nothing could be worse than no freedom."

"How about no Christopher?" I said.

"What kind of life would it be for Christopher? All the good things you have now you'd be leaving behind."

I spent a morning researching at New York University's law library. All countries except Brazil have an extradition policy with the United States. Would taking Christopher out of the country be kidnapping?

I looked up other cases, particularly the Baby Lenore adoption. A Colombian woman living in New York had given permission to the Spence–Chapin agency in New York to place her newborn daughter for adoption. The adoptive parents, an attorney and his wife from the Bronx, named the baby Lenore. Ten days after the birth, the biological mother told Spence–Chapin she wanted the child. The agency balked at passing the information along to the couple. When the adoptive parents finally heard the bad news, they took the case to court. The couple lost in all three of New York's courts. Their attorney suggested to them that they file for adoption in Florida, a state known to be more lenient to adoptive parents. The couple and Lenore relocated in Florida and were successful in their lawsuit; the decision was overturned. Unfortunately for us, this case inspired the creation of the Interstate Compact, specifically to avoid a repeat of the Baby Lenore situation. Now states must respect each others' custody decisions and are not empowered to reverse them.

Would we run away with Christopher? I knew how much Jeremy enjoyed having his own practice, how important his work was to him. We both thrived in New York. I couldn't imagine the three of us hiding out in some motel in Oklahoma, or living on a coffee plantation in Brazil. I'd been so nervous when I thought the process server was pursuing me. Imagine the uncertainty, the tenuousness, of life underground.

CHAPTER

Six

Our initial appearance before Judge Finberg was on July 9, our fourth wedding anniversary. We drove in from the cottage on Long Island Sound to rush hour in a sweltering New York City. Jeremy and I changed from shorts to suits in the bathroom of the babysitter's studio apartment. Out-of-town friends were staying in our loft for the week, which was Jeremy's official summer vacation, and I didn't want to involve them by going home. I told the babysitter we'd call when we had an idea of how long our business appointment would be. Christopher babbled happily from her arms as we waved good-bye.

The Family Court building in lower Manhattan is a black marble fortress. In the seating area outside the courtrooms, the chairs are bolted to the floor, as if in an attempt to impose order on peoples' lives. Everyone there knows that everyone else there has big problems.

In a strange way, I had begun to look forward to going to court. An upcoming court date was entered in my calendar in pen. No tentative pencil used here; no chance of cancellation if it rained too hard or Christopher had a nasty cough. If court was on Wednesday, Christopher wouldn't host the play group. If court was on Thursday, I'd do my freelance work on Friday.

Wearing my gray tweed suit made me feel confident. My regular mother's attire was a sweatsuit and sneakers. I hoped the judge would see me as a young professional mother, a refined person with morals, someone like her own daughter. The only good mother for Christopher.

Angelina was already in the waiting area, alone, sitting very still, reading a Spanish *Reader's Digest*. Her long wavy hair shrouded her from real scrutiny; periodically she'd lift a hand and toss it back over her shoulder. Her serenity reminded me of lines from Hesse's *Siddhartha*: "I can sit. I can wait. I can fast." It had taken her a year to get to New York. What were a few hours in a courtroom?

In any situation that demands indefinite waiting, I find order in editing the contents of my purse. Chris's half-eaten rice cake, Trident cinnamon gum wrappers, the movie section from last Sunday's Long Island newspaper, an expired Pampers coupon.

Norman rushed in, dropped his briefcase in the seat next to Jeremy's, and said, "Be right back. Gotta make a phone call."

Norman had told us there was no sure way of knowing exactly what would happen that day. The trial could be over in a few hours. If we were allowed to bring in witnesses, it could stretch out. The judge held the reins of power.

Nat Schwartz and Jorge Cabas, the interpreter, walked in together and sat down with Angelina for a few minutes. Then Norman and Schwartz stood by the windows to confer. Their laughter was jarring, but we came to realize that their antagonistic courtroom behavior turned into camaraderie beyond earshot of the judge's bench.

Intermittently a uniformed guard would emerge from the courtroom and call in a new case. Most of the plaintiffs were teenaged boys who looked uncomfortable in their ill-fitting jackets, probably borrowed for their court date. After an hour or so, the guard announced that court would be adjourned until two o'clock. Jeremy and I celebrated our anniversary by lunching in nearby Chinatown. "I'm glad I asked you to marry me," I told Jeremy over General Tso's chicken. "Me, too," he said, "but what a way to spend an anniversary."

Back in Family Court, we waited another hour. Norman paced back and forth, popping Velamints and making phone calls. I marveled at Angelina's continued stillness. My sandals chafed my bare feet; I should have worn stockings. I longed to be back on the beach with Christopher. When we were the only ones left in the waiting area, the guard called, "Rodriguez versus Ryan." Norman, Schwartz, Angelina, Jeremy, and I filed into the small courtroom. Jorge Cabas had not returned after the lunch break; anyway, the courtroom was closed to the public. The guard directed us to sit behind two long tables facing the bench. There was no gallery. Judge Finberg entered from a separate doorway behind the bench. The guard instructed us to rise and identify ourselves for the stenographer, who sat poised behind her little machine, already looking bored on this hot summer afternoon. Jeremy and Marguerite Ryan, adoptive father, adoptive mother; Angelina Rodriguez, natural mother. (I wince at "natural mother"; it's so qualitative. Is "adoptive mother" *un*natural, less good? "Birth mother" or "biological mother" is more equitable.)

Norman told us we were lucky to have gotten Millicent Finberg. She was the best possible judge for our case—

the most liberal, the one most in favor of adoptive parents. Her appearance was deceptive. She was slight, almost frail, at least in her mid-sixties. The ruffled collar of her lavender blouse sprouted up from her black judicial robe like a flower. Her rumpled brown hair was worn in Mamie Eisenhower bangs. High cheekbones offset her big blue eyes, giving her face a gaunt look. When she spoke, it was with a slow Southern drawl.

Judge Finberg took a careful look at each of us. Then she made a rambling statement consolidating the two legal issues before the court. The petitioner, Angelina, was hoping to gain custody of Christopher. The respondents, Jeremy and I, were hoping to adopt Christopher and to dispense with Angelina's consent.

Judge Finberg said that she would first consider the nature of the documents that Angelina had signed and then consider the question of whether a voluntary consent had been signed. If she were to determine that a voluntary consent had been signed, she would then decide whether revocation of this consent would be allowed, based on whether the best interests of Christopher would be served by permitting revocation.

I hung on the judge's words, straining to concentrate. Angelina frowned and chewed her bottom lip as she listened to the interpreter's murmur. The only other sound in the room was the crack of the guard's gum chewing.

"Refusing to view a consent as valid solely because it is made before the child is born may be quite contrary to the interest of child welfare," said the judge. "I think it is unanimously agreed that if a child is to be placed for adoption, the sooner the child is placed for adoption the better it is for the welfare of the child.

"I think it would be appropriate to commence with the issue of what consents, if any, the petitioner did give and under what circumstances she gave them. That would of course entail her understanding at the time of what was transpiring."

"Your Honor, if I may be heard?" requested Norman.

Judge Finberg said yes.

He said, "I have made diligent efforts to locate the Ryans' California attorney, Neil Hernandez. It was not until two minutes before we walked into this hearing that we were finally able to reach him. I have sent telegrams, called him from midnight our time to six o'clock in the morning, and it was just now that I was able to reach him. I did not have time to go fully into the circumstances or the nature of the documents that he prepared for signature. I think before I can adequately prepare to proceed with the determination of the facts, because this case is so complicated, because of the nature of the documents prepared out there and as to their interpretation, that I really request an adjournment of one week in order that I can interview these people—the Ryans' attorney and the hospital social worker. I do not want to delay the case. My clients want it resolved as soon as anybody, but I will need California witnesses in here."

Schwartz jumped to his feet. "May I be heard? Your Honor, when I first got involved in this matter I had the feeling that an injustice would be done no matter what the outcome of this case to the parties. Mr. Bernstein says to this Court he needs a week's adjournment. It is amazing how he stalls this case."

Judge Finberg said, "I can't very well join in a conclusion that Mr. and Mrs. Ryan or this attorney or their California attorney were stalling this matter when a petition for habeas corpus was filed and when, unfortunately for the petitioner, the California Court decided that it was the wrong type of remedy for her to pursue.

"Unfortunately, as those who are accustomed to being

in this court know, we have very, very crowded calendars, and it is difficult to hold any proceeding in a continuous fashion. I believe that Miss Rodriguez's direct testimony should be taken today and that if Mr. Bernstein wishes to reserve his right to cross-examination he will be justified in asking for a continuance for that purpose. I have looked at all the documents relating to the release of the child and I find them somewhat ambiguous."

Angelina Octavia Rodriguez was sworn in through an official Spanish interpreter. Schwartz led her through some basic historical information. Her age: "I am already thirty. I was born in 1952." How long had she been in the United States: "Since 1979." How many family members she had in El Salvador: "We are eight brothers and sisters and my mother." Her work in California: "I looked after the three children in the Arnaldo home. I cleaned the house."

Schwartz asked Angelina when she first spoke to someone concerning her pregnancy. She wrinkled her brow, sighed, then said, "With the lady where I work. I told her that perhaps I was like that because I was not feeling well. Then she went to the drugstore and purchased something for an analysis and it came to her I was."

Schwartz said, "When you learned you were pregnant did you have any discussions with regard to what you were going to do with the child if and when it was born?"

Angelina replied, "Mrs. Arnaldo said something about an adoption. Her intentions were to help me. That is, she did not say it trying to convince me of it but that it could be done."

"And did there come a time that Mr. or Mrs. Arnaldo spoke of friends of theirs, the Ryans, in New York?"

"Well, yes," said Angelina. "A friend of theirs told them about the Ryan family."

Schwartz then asked Angelina to look at the Interstate

Compact application and verify her signature. This document had been prepared by Neil Hernandez when Angelina was six months pregnant. It read, in part:

> I have carefully considered the matter and it is my desire and decision to place for adoption whatever child or children to whom I give birth. It is my wish and I hereby consent that my child or children be placed for adoption with the aforementioned Mr. and Mrs. Jeremy Ryan. It is also my wish and I hereby consent further that upon the birth of my child or children, the aforementioned Mr. and Mrs. Ryan assume custody and control of the same pending finalization of adoption proceedings, which I am informed and believe will take place in the State of New York.

"Can you tell us the facts that took place just before and leading up to your signing that document?" asked Schwartz.

"Well, I felt confused."

"Go on."

"I was confused."

"I don't believe that was an answer to the question," Judge Finberg said.

"I am not asking what was on her mind," said Schwartz. "I am asking her who she spoke to and how she came to actually sign that particular paper." He walked up next to Angelina's witness chair and said to her, "Did you know that by signing that document you were giving the Ryans your child to be born later?"

Angelina replied, "After being born, yes, but temporarily."

Then Schwartz led Angelina through the three months remaining between her signing that document and Christopher's birth in July. Through his church, Neil Hernandez had found a *pro bono* lawyer, Mike Cole, for Angelina.

Schwartz said, "You called Mr. Hernandez when you went into the hospital?"

"Yes."

"Did you see anyone at the hospital?"

"Did I see anyone?"

Patiently, Schwartz suggested, "Any lawyers or the Ryans or anybody like that?"

"I saw Hernandez."

"When did you see him?"

"On the seventeenth."

"The day after your son was born?"

"Yes."

"And were you in bed at the time?"

"Yes."

"And do you recall what your conversation that day concerned?"

"Yes, I remember."

"Can you tell us what you said to Mr. Hernandez and what he said to you?"

"Well, I wanted to see the Ryan family, but he said it is better like this in order not to let it seem so sad."

"When he said it is better like this he said it was better for you not to see the Ryans?"

"Yes, so that things would not become emotional."

"Now," said Schwartz, "did you sign any documents that day in the hospital, the seventeenth, when Mr. Hernandez came to see you?"

The placement-for-adoption form created by Neil read:

> . . . do hereby place for adoption with Mr. and Mrs. Jeremy and Marguerite Ryan. . . . I understand that this declaration is not a consent to adoption and in signing this document I retain my legal rights to the custody, control, earnings, and support of said child.

"On the seventeenth did you read that document to yourself in Spanish or did Mr. Hernandez read it to you in Spanish?" asked Schwartz.

"Yes, I read this," replied Angelina.

"And was it your intent at the time you signed that document that this was only a temporary situation? You were giving up your son at that point to the Ryans?"

"Yes."

"That is about all I have, Your Honor," said Schwartz.

It was five o'clock, time to adjourn. Court always adjourned exactly on time. Our next court date was set for three weeks later. It was becoming clear what Judge Finberg meant when she said it was difficult to hold hearings in a continuous fashion.

Three weeks later, Schwartz decided to continue his direct examination of Angelina.

"Did there come a time that you went to a lawyer's office to regain your son?"

"Yes," said Angelina, "I went to him."

"Which—to whom?"

"I went to Hernandez's office."

"After the telephone call?"

"Yes, I went to the lawyer Miguel Posito."

"Did you go to the lawyer who was supposedly representing you, Mr. Cole?"

"Yes, I went so the child would be returned."

"Who did you see first, lawyer Cole or lawyer Hernandez?"

"First I saw Cole and later I went to the office of Miguel Posito."

"Who is Miguel Posito?"

"He was the lawyer that represented me over there."

"And are you telling us that you are no longer represented by Mr. Cole, the lawyer?"

"Mr. Cole represented me."

"How was it that you came to have lawyer Cole and later Mr. Posito?"

"From right there, from Mr. Cole, he recommended that they could help me."

"In other words, Mr. Cole recommended Mr. Posito?"

"Yes."

"Was it Mr. Cole himself, or someone in his office?"

"The interpreter."

"Mr. Cole had an interpreter?"

Apparently what had happened, according to Neil Hernandez, was that when the *pro bono* attorney, Mike Cole, found out that Angelina was withholding her consent, he was not willing to represent her anymore. His interpreter recommended her to a Miguel Posito in a Legal Aid type of place for Hispanics.

Angelina said, "We spoke with Hernandez about the fact that I wanted my child back. He said he was going to let the lawyer from New York know so that my child would be returned. He said the Ryan family wasn't going to allow—wasn't going to give me the child voluntarily, that possibly they would not give it to me, that I would have to speak with them. Miguel Posito took my case so that my child would be returned."

Schwartz asked, "What did you do when you learned that you could not be successful in California?"

"Then I tried to come over here, but I had no place and the lawyer didn't know anyone. But in the end somebody gave me a room to stay in."

"Is that somebody Mr. Jorge Cabas?"

"Yes, Jorge Cabas. A friend of Miguel Posito knows Jorge Cabas's family, and Miguel Posito asked them if I could come over here and they said yes. And that's how I happen to be here."

"And sometime thereafter Mr. Cabas introduced you to me?"

"Yes."

"I have no further questions," Schwartz said.

Norman began his cross-examination by asking Angelina her purpose in coming to the United States. "I came here. I wanted to better myself, to work, to help my family."

"What type of visa did you come here with?"

Schwartz leapt to his feet. "Objection," he yelled. "Your Honor, I'm going to ask the Court for a direction on the basis that I feel an answer to that might incriminate her with regard to another proceeding."

Judge Finberg said, "If the attorney states in good faith that he believes that she might incriminate herself, I assume for the purpose of a deportation hearing . . ."

"Correct, Your Honor," said Schwartz.

Norman interjected, "Your Honor, I believe that the issue of status, the purpose, the documents that were signed—this whole case seems to border on the signing of various documents and purposes. And I think it's highly important to know what Miss Rodriguez signed when coming to the United States, what she said there, whether she understood that."

Judge Finberg said, "I think that while a deportation proceeding is not, strictly speaking, a criminal proceeding, it would certainly be my inclination to hold that she can invoke the privilege if she wishes to. Now, I think an inference can be drawn that there is at least the possibility of a deportation proceeding. I think there is another question—"

Schwartz interrupted, "May I just state to the Court—"

"I'm not saying, of course, that there will be," said the judge, "but I think I have to give some thought to the

the question of if there were to be a deportation proceeding—"

Schwartz tried again. "May I just say something, Your Honor?"

The judge continued, "—how that would affect this case?"

Schwartz insisted, "I have information that, indeed, there were no documents signed."

"Of course no document was signed," Jeremy whispered to me, "she probably snuck over the Mexican border."

Judge Finberg said, "I think the testimony that seems to the attorneys to be relevant should be taken so that we can finish with this hearing and the legal arguments should follow, rather than take up our time with the legal arguments at this point."

Norman continued, "Miss Rodriguez, how long after coming to the United States did you first seek and obtain employment?"

"What was the question?" said Angelina. "How many times?"

"No. How long after coming—?"

"Excuse me," said the interpreter, "she doesn't seem to understand the question. May I repeat it?"

"Sure," said Norman.

"Two times," answered Angelina.

"Two months?" asked Schwartz.

Judge Finberg said, "Two jobs."

Norman sighed. "In what month did you come to the United States?"

"I came in July. I don't remember the date."

"In July of 1979?"

"Uh-huh."

"In what month did you first start working in the United States?"

"I started around three months after. I don't remember too well."

Judge Finberg said, "Excuse me. I don't really see any relevance to this testimony."

Norman was trying to establish that Angelina didn't pay taxes on her earnings, but Judge Finberg sustained Schwartz's objections.

Norman then pursued another angle, asking Angelina what she understood an adoption to be. "I understand—well, that adoption is to give the child to another family. The other family are the parents."

Had she ever discussed adoption with Eileen Conroy, asked Norman. "Yes, we spoke about this, that the child could possibly be given to the Ryan family and that the child was going to be happy there."

When Norman asked Angelina about her conversations with the hospital social worker, Angelina denied that Pat Henderson had mentioned alternatives, such as foster care. Angelina described her meeting with Pat after giving birth: "She would ask me if I was feeling well. I would tell her that I was feeling well, but in my heart I wasn't feeling well."

Before we recessed for the day, Judge Finberg said, "I have one brief question I was going to ask Miss Rodriguez just to clarify one thing that she said. Miss Rodriguez, I think you said that you came to the United States so you could help your family. Would you tell us who you were referring to as your family?"

Angelina said, "My mother—" She started to cry.

Judge Finberg said, "Well, I'm sorry. I didn't mean to upset you. You were speaking of your family in Salvador."

"Yes."

"You have some family there besides your mother?"

"My mother, my sisters, my brothers—"

"Would you want to say what caused you to cry?"

"Yes. I want to have my son."

"I see. All right. Has your family said anything about that?"

"They don't know."

"You mean they don't know that you have a child?"

"No, because I didn't want to tell them so that they wouldn't worry because they love me a great deal and I love them. And if they realize what's happened to me, they are going to worry a great deal."

Judge Finberg said, "The Court could continue this tomorrow afternoon if you are available."

"Your Honor," Schwartz said, "I must state for the record that I'm on trial in Nassau County, as I told the Court the last time."

The date was July 28; our next hearing was set for October 2.

My mother spent August with us on Long Island. I have inherited from her a strong fear of—and developed my own allergy to—cats, who seem to pick up my fearful vibrations. Once when visiting friends in the country, we were dining by candlelight while their two Siamese cats minced back and forth over the stone mantlepiece of the fireplace behind my back. Periodically I'd cast a glance backwards at the cats, but the blaze of their firelit eyes made me drop my look first. The dinner progressed with laughter, storytelling, and wine. I finally relaxed enough to forget the cats. Even my sneezing had subsided. All of a sudden, the bigger cat pounced from the mantle onto my shoulder. I screamed and bolted from my chair. Everyone at the table collapsed with laughter.

So when two small cats and their mother appeared on our cottage porch one August morning, my mother and I were alarmed. Christopher, however, squealed in delight and grabbed for their tails. The next day the mother and four little cats came back. Then the mother disappeared and didn't return, but the little ones stayed.

I took a firm policy. No cats in the house. As we stood in the A&P checkout line with a five-pound bag of cat vittles, I said to my mother, "If my friends in Connecticut could see me now, they would never let me live this down."

I sat at the table on the porch doing my freelance copyediting. Every several minutes a few cats would scurry by, followed by Christopher clomp-clomping in the red leather shoes my mother had bought him at the shoestore in town. My mother, her back beginning to stoop with osteoporosis, brought up the rear of this ragtag parade. Around and around they went. Such moments made me wish I could crystallize Christopher, keep him at this age and stage forever.

When Labor Day came and we packed up to go back to the city, I called the local ASPCA. "You city people are all alike," sighed the voice at the other end. "You just abandon these poor creatures. We're full; we can't take any more." So we bought another big bag of cat food and dribbled it down the trail toward the public beach, hoping that some townspeople might want to pick up the cats. As we headed back up the path to the cottage, the mother cat strolled onto the porch. "You came back," I said excitedly. "C'mon, down to the beach. Your children are waiting."

CHAPTER

Seven

Norman continued his cross-examination in October. "You testified prior to today that you discovered your pregnancy after taking a test with something that Mrs. Arnaldo had obtained from a drugstore. When did that occur, madam?"

Angelina concentrated. "That was—I don't remember very well, but around October."

"And how soon after taking that test did you go to see a doctor about your pregnancy? To be examined?"

"I don't remember exactly, but I believe in January. I went to San Francisco General Hospital."

Norman walked up quite close to Angelina's chair, smiled at her, then half-turned away from her. "After first discovering you were pregnant through the test, did you ever contemplate aborting your child?"

"Objection," said Schwartz instantly.

Judge Finberg said to Angelina, "You may answer the question. It is overruled on the basis that I believe the question of the intent permeates this case and anything that would reflect upon the intent would have some pertinence here, counsel. Please answer."

"No," said Angelina, "I didn't want to have an abortion."

"Why not?"

"Because I wanted to have my child."

Norman said, "When, after discovering that you were pregnant, did you first discuss adoption?"

"Objection. Asked and answered, Your Honor," said Schwartz.

"I don't think so, Your Honor," said Norman.

"I don't believe so either, counsel," said the judge. "Look, I will permit it. Unfortunately this has been fragmented and rather dragged out, and I am not quite positive. Proceed."

"In what month?" asked Norman.

The frown again. Angelina said, "I don't remember exactly, but I was about four or five months pregnant then."

"When you were four months pregnant, madam, did you make a decision to sever your ties with your child after it was born?"

Angelina looked down at her lap. She answered slowly in a barely audible voice. "I accepted, I made it, but I did it because I thought that way he could have the very best, but I made a mistake."

Holding out the placement-for-adoption document, Norman said, "Miss Rodriguez, in the first paragraph there, you state that you are placing your child for adoption with the Ryans. The next paragraph states, however, that you are not consenting to the adoption. Would you please explain to the Court here what it was that you thought you were doing when you signed this document with regard to the adoption?"

Schwartz's objection was overruled.

"To give him," said Angelina.

"No further questions," said Norman.

"To give him," said Judge Finberg, "what do you mean, to give him, madam?"

"The child, to the Ryans."

"For what?" asked the judge.

"For adoption."

Judge Finberg turned to Schwartz. "Any redirect examination, counsel?"

Schwartz looked upset. He walked up close to Angelina's chair, leaned on the arm, and said to her, "The document we are talking about, madam"—he handed it to her—"can you see the date upon it?"

Angelina said, "Oh, yes."

"Did you think we were just now referring to another document?"

"Objection, Your Honor," said Norman. "The witness saw the document herself."

Judge Finberg said, "Yes, I can't permit that kind of back and forth and up and down and rehabilitation, counsel. Madam, if you realized that this document was dated in fact July 17, would you have given any different answers to the questions asked of you by counsel?"

"No."

"Your Honor," said Schwartz, "she was looking at the language and not at the date and quite frankly—"

"Look, counsel," said Judge Finberg, "I have no reason to believe that Miss Rodriguez is incompetent. She is being treated in this proceeding as a competent witness, as compared to someone who is unable to testify because of a state of mental confusion, which prevents that person from being able to respond to questions. Now, on that basis, counsel, if she is presented with a document and if she appears to be looking at that particular document, particularly under the circumstances I just mentioned to you, of the translator pointing it out, line by line to her, her answers as to that document have to be given some credence by the Court. It is not possible to conduct this proceeding on the basis of a lawyer then standing up and saying, 'But she didn't know what she was testifying to.' If you wish to argue at the end of the proceeding that her testimony should not be given any weight because she is too confused or something of that sort or you want to bring in witnesses to show that she is in a state of mental confusion, then you may do so, counsel, but until that is done, I will indulge in the presumption that she is a competent person and is able to testify. Are we finished with this witness?"

I was supposed to take the stand next, but Eileen Conroy, in New York with her husband on business, agreed to testify. Eileen looked responsible on the witness stand, prim in her navy flowered dress, vulnerable, her arms plump above the elbows, her brown hair curled so it bounced when she nodded. She was the pretty, well-scrubbed type of woman who giggled a lot, who had seemingly boundless energy and enthusiasm, who gave homemaking—with her talents for gardening and decorating—a real dignity. Eileen and her husband, Dan, had one biological daughter and one adopted daughter. After failing to conceive a second time, Eileen had gone about the adoption purposefully, writing to several gynecologists in Ireland. A doctor with the same maiden name as Eileen's, Maher, had produced her letter when confronted by a tearfully pregnant young woman whose intended husband hadn't shown up for the wedding.

Norman asked Eileen to describe her involvement in our situation. "My neighbor called me and said Angelina was pregnant, that she wanted to have her baby adopted.

Since I spoke Spanish and I had adopted a child myself, she asked me did I know of some people that might be potential adoptive parents."

"In February of 1982," said Norman, "did you have a conversation with Ms. Rodriguez?"

"Yes."

"And what was that conversation? What did she say to you and what did you say to her in that conversation?"

"I translated a letter written by the Ryans to Mr. Arnaldo."

"Did she make any statement regarding her desire to place her child for adoption with the Ryans?"

"Yes, I believe it was left that she wanted to proceed with adoption."

Schwartz objected.

Judge Finberg said, "Can you to the best of your recollection tell the Court what her exact words were?"

"Well, you see," said Eileen, "we were having a discussion and she seemed extremely interested in pursuing the Ryans. When she left, I believe, they were going to—"

"Objection to what they were going to do," said Schwartz.

Judge Finberg said to Eileen, "I'm sorry. Go ahead."

Norman asked, "Did Ms. Rodriguez say anything to you that she—did she give you any statements as to what her feelings about the Ryans were?"

Eileen said, "Definitely. She gave me the impression that she wanted the adoption proceedings to continue with the Ryans."

"Now, just a minute," said the judge. "Perhaps I should speak to Ms. Conroy a moment. Ms. Conroy, you probably are not accustomed to, or perhaps you never have, testified in court. Well, the rule is, as far as you can possibly recall, to state the exact words that were spoken to you by the other person. The reason for that, I think you will see, is that if you speak in terms of your impressions or what you thought the other person thought or something of that sort, it is much more vague and you might be wrong or you might be right in your impression. So that if you state to the best of your recall what words were stated by the person you're referring to, then the Court can decide."

Eileen looked exasperated. "She came to my house to have me translate this letter because she wanted her baby—"

"*Ob-jec-tion*," said Schwartz, as if it were three words.

Kindly, patiently, as if speaking to a child, Judge Finberg said, "Well, now, I know it's a little difficult for you. 'Because she wanted,' for example, is just the kind of thing that is objected to. If you said, 'Because she said,' or, 'She said such and such and I said such and such,' that would be the best way to testify about this matter."

"She said she wanted the Ryans to adopt her baby," said Eileen.

Norman asked Eileen to describe her hospital visit to Angelina the day of Christopher's birth. "I went at eleven o'clock at night; I stayed until two-thirty. I went home and I went back at six o'clock in the morning. The baby was born at noon."

"Were you there when Ms. Rodriguez delivered the child?"

"Yes."

"And did she say something to you at that time right after the delivery?"

"She wanted to know if the baby was OK and she was extremely happy that everything was OK and that, you know, she was mainly interested in the baby."

Eileen had then gone home, but she returned to the hospital the next day. "She was in very good spirits. She was pleased to hear that the Ryans had come and that the baby was being snuggled and cuddled and all the rest and given the bottle."

"Objection."

"What did she say to you," instructed Norman, "not your observations."

"She asked me, 'Are the Ryans happy?' I said, 'They seem to be thrilled. They are absolutely thrilled. They couldn't be happier.' And she wanted to know if he was beautiful, if I had seen him yet, and I said yes."

Norman asked Eileen to tell about when she learned Angelina had changed her mind.

"I told her I had been in New York and I had seen the Ryans. I had seen Christopher. They were devastated by this news that she had changed her mind and their hearts were broken. She said she understood but that she wanted her baby back."

"Was anything else said in that conversation?" Norman asked.

Eileen replied, "I said how Christopher was established with the Ryans, you know—teddy bears and all the rest. That their hearts were absolutely broken, and we discussed that. And she—" Eileen began to cry. I noticed that Angelina and the interpreter, a cool-looking woman of perhaps fifty, were holding hands under the defense table. The stenographer wiped her eyes with her hand.

"Would you like some water?" asked Norman.

"I'm all right. I'm sorry."

"Do you want a five-minute recess?" Schwartz asked.

"I'm fine," Eileen said. "It's OK."

Judge Finberg peered at Eileen over her shaded eyeglasses and said, "It's an emotional matter."

Norman continued, "After you stated that, did Ms. Rodriguez state anything to you?"

"Yes, she said that her decision had been out of almost a whim."

Schwartz objected quickly.

"Your Honor—" Norman interjected.

"Overruled," said the judge. "That's what she said; that's what she said."

"I can say it in Spanish if you want," offered Eileen.

"Was anything else said that day?" asked Norman.

"I said, 'It is a shame,' and it was left at a standstill. I simply talked to her for a while."

Schwartz began aggressively. "Was your adoption in New York or California?" he asked Eileen.

"California."

"Did you ever tell Miss Rodriguez she could change her mind later?"

"No."

"And in fact can you change your mind in the state of California?" asked Schwartz.

"Yes," Eileen replied, "but it never came up, the decision to change her mind. Afterwards she did it."

"I believe I'm entitled to an answer to my question."

"I think you got an answer, Mr. Schwartz," Judge Finberg said.

Schwartz countered, "Your Honor has allowed this witness to discuss a myriad number of observations. Now I ask a simple question as to whether or not she told her whether she could change her mind, and the witness herself claims that she told this witness all about adoption."

"She never claimed that," the judge said wearily. "Mr. Schwartz, seriously, there is no objection to anything you wanted to ask. There is no need for oratory here and there is certainly no need for misquoting the witness. The witness did not say she told Ms. Rodriguez 'all about adoption.' And so I think that we can proceed better if you are a little more careful about your quotations of the witness's testimony."

Politely, Schwartz said, "You told us a little while ago that you informed her about private placement adoptions and institutional adoptions?"

"Yes. I did not say I told her all about it."

Judge Finberg leaned toward Eileen. "Just a minute. Another thing: Let me tell you another rule that should be observed. Just answer the questions; don't volunteer any information."

Schwartz asked, "And did you tell her about a time period within which a biological mother has to change her mind?"

"Just yes or no," suggested the judge.

"Yes."

"And how long did you say it was?"

"In discussing the Children's Home Society, I told her the baby was placed at four months of age."

"That wasn't the question," Judge Finberg interjected.

"That's what came up," was Eileen's reply.

Judge Finberg said, "I don't believe the witness understands your question, but if you wish to pursue, you can make it clearer to her."

Schwartz looked genuinely puzzled. "She paused for a good deal of time and contemplated before answering the question."

"Just proceed," said the judge.

Schwartz resumed his questioning of Eileen. "Did you speak to her specifically with regard to the time period within which a mother has to change her mind—"

"Yes," Eileen replied quickly.

Frustrated, Schwartz said, "Would you wait until I complete my question?—In connection with a private placement adoption?"

"No."

"Do you know the period in California?"

"Yes."

"What is the period in California? Did you ever tell her about it?"

"Objection, Your Honor," said Norman. "She already answered that she did not tell her."

Judge Finberg nodded. "She's answered."

"Did you tell her about any time?" said Schwartz.

"No."

"Was there a reason for your not telling her?"

"No."

"You failed to tell her? You neglected to tell her?"

"No, it never—"

"What is the answer? What is the time period?"

"Adoptions are finalized after six months in California."

"Up until that time a person has the right to change her mind?"

Judge Finberg sighed in exasperation. "You refuse to let the witness answer the question of whether she knows what the law is with regard to revocation of consent. The fact that it takes up to six months to finalize an adoption does not necessarily mean the biological parent has a right to revoke consent during six months. It certainly doesn't mean that in New York, and I have no reason to think it means so in California. I don't—I simply can't sit by when the witness is asked a question which she obviously doesn't understand."

"Maybe she does," said Schwartz. "Do you know how long you have to revoke the consent in the state of California?"

Eileen answered, "Six months."

"Six months to revoke the consent? Is that to the best of your knowledge?"

"Yes, I guess so."

"Did you tell—"

"Six months during—"

"—Knowing that you never told Ms. Rodriguez that she had an opportunity to revoke—"

"Objection," said Norman. "That's been asked and answered several times, Your Honor."

Judge Finberg said, "This is cross-examination, and I think that it can be answered in the context with the answer of the other question. However, it's the Court's opinion that the witness does not understand the question that was asked her."

Schwartz said, "At any time in conversations in June or July did you ever inform her about the time period within which she could change her mind?"

Judge Finberg began rummaging through the contents of the enormous black handbag she always carried into court with her. She pulled out a newspaper and scanned it for a few minutes, as if the interrogation had become so irrelevant that there was no point in her listening.

Eileen said, "She knew fully well when she made this decision she could change her mind. I did not apprise her of legalities because I was not her lawyer."

Judge Finberg looked up sharply from her newspaper and said, "You said she knew she could change her mind. Did she say something to you?"

"Our discussions in June and July were about whether she still wanted to have her baby adopted, and she continually said, 'I have kept my decision. I have not changed my mind.' "

Schwartz said, "And when you said to her it would be easier to change her mind now, to use your words, did you mean—excuse me, madam—did you mean for her or for the prospective adoptive parents?"

"Everyone."

"For everyone." Schwartz paused. "Is that the language you used? 'Everyone. It would be easier for everyone.' Was that the language you used here?"

Eileen said, "I said to her, 'It would be easier if you are going to change your mind, it would be easier for everyone concerned that you do it now rather than breaking hearts.' That was a tremendous responsibility."

"Objection to that last part as not responsive," said Schwartz.

"Well, I think the testimony is getting quite repetitive," said the judge.

"He was obnoxious," Eileen said to her husband over dinner that evening with Jeremy and me. "Schwartz was simply obnoxious."

"I guess that's his job," said Dan.

"I've heard," said Jeremy, "that a lawyer is never supposed to ask a witness a question unless he knows what the answer will be."

I was both dreading and looking forward to testifying, but my turn was put off again because Pat Henderson, the California hospital social worker, was able to fly in from San Francisco for our next court date. Judge Finberg was now scheduling us after lunch, at 2:00 P.M., as it had apparently become clear that we were not to be a quickly resolved case.

I had remembered Pat in San Francisco as being mousy—dressed casually in corduroy trousers, with long, straight hair and wire-rimmed glasses. Today she looked professional—a skirted suit, curled hair, no glasses, carefully applied makeup. She was polite but cool to Jeremy and me, obviously wishing to appear impartial.

Norman led her through her qualifications and her role in the hospital. "I provide counseling and evaluation services for the young women who are coming into the

Obstetrics Clinic. The counseling covers—when someone is unsure about what their plans are for their baby—letting them know about community resources, agencies, basically to help them to determine what services are best available for them in the community."

Norman discussed the day after Christopher's birth: "Other than vacillating as to whether or not to see the Ryans or the child, did she give any indication of vacillating on her decision to surrender her child for adoption?"

"No, she seemed very, very firm on her decision to relinquish."

Later, Norman said, "What was her emotional state when she signed the hospital release form?"

"She was talking about feelings of sadness but she kept coming back to feeling it was the best decision both for herself and for her child and she talked about the quality of the home."

Schwartz had been unusually quiet during Norman's direct examination. The only thing he objected to was Pat Henderson's being accepted as an expert witness, which meant that Norman could ask her opinion on some points. Judge Finberg overruled the objection and Pat was qualified as an expert.

Norman's last question to Pat was, "Do you believe, again in your expert opinion, that she made a knowing, intelligent, and voluntary decision to surrender her child for adoption as opposed to surrendering her child for temporary care?"

"Yes," Pat stated firmly. "I believe that she did make that decision knowingly and voluntarily."

Schwartz began by asking Pat who had paid for her trip. She answered that Jeremy and I had paid for her plane fare; the hospital had paid for her time. Luckily for us, she had stayed with a friend in Brooklyn and spared us a hotel bill.

Schwartz then asked Pat about Angelina. "And would you say that her main concern was that she felt her inability to financially support the family, was that the subject of your conversations?"

"No," Pat answered. "She and I, when we were speaking, also had talked about both concrete and emotional issues. She felt that a child needed two parents and that the baby's father was not willing or able to help her out. She felt that the child deserved a better home than she felt able to provide."

In his redirect, Norman said, "Based on your observations of Miss Rodriguez, your conversations and meeting with her during her stay in the hospital, is it your opinion that Miss Rodriguez's intent when she signed both the hospital release form and the papers for the attorney, that it was her clear intent, madam, to surrender her child for adoption?"

"Objection," said Schwartz. "The papers speak for themselves. They are not adoption forms."

"Overruled," said the judge. "I have read the papers, and I am not going to give my opinion about the papers until the case is concluded. They certainly would sustain the possibility of an argument that they are sufficiently ambiguous. So the testimony as to the intent of the signer might be relevant to an argument with respect to the meaning of the papers."

"Things are going great," said Norman as we stood in the marbled lobby of the Family Court building. "I think we can build a good case on parole evidence." Judge Finberg had made frequent references to the fact that she found the documents Angelina signed ambiguous. Norman told us that if a document is considered sufficiently unclear, the spoken evidence may be more important than the document. In this regard, it was helpful to have Eileen's and Pat's testimony bear out Angelina's firm intent for adoption.

Norman suggested that we investigate whether or not Angelina was involved in any questionable activities. Unfitness, according to him, was most often illustrated by drug addiction or some other very specific, measurable moral deficiency. We hired a detective to trail Angelina for several hours. Over a period of two days of observation, the detective reported that Angelina had sat on the stoop of the tenement in the Bronx and had gone to the grocery store. He charged us $1,000 for procuring this information; Jeremy paid him $500. Angelina seemed an unlikely candidate for angel dust or needle-marked arms.

CHAPTER
Eight

Two weeks later, Neil Hernandez flew in from San Francisco to testify. He agreed to stay in our loft. We gave him our bedroom, the only space in our home with four walls around it, for privacy. In the morning, Christopher found the closed bedroom door irresistible, and I had to keep chasing him, dragging him away so that Neil could sleep.

It was strange to have Neil staying in our home. He was Jeremy's and my age, mid-thirties, and a comfortable, casual enough person. But there had been an undercurrent during our lengthy talks before Chris's birth, and stray comments of his kept coming back to me now, during the trial. "I think it's best for a mother to keep her child if she possibly can" had been one of these. I wondered now if Neil had acted completely in our best interests or whether he had felt some bond to Angelina that ultimately could have led him to protect her legally instead of us. She had told him he reminded her of the priest she confided in. What else had they said to each other?

I'd put Neil in touch with the New York social worker who conducted a home study of Jeremy and me months before Christopher's birth, and she in turn had sent him New York Family Court consent forms. But he'd chosen to prepare his own forms, chosen to include that damning clause that said Angelina was not consenting. Why hadn't that language bothered Jeremy and me when Neil showed us the form the day after Christopher's birth? We accepted the document that Angelina would sign without perceiving it as restrictive or dangerous. Had we been too excited about Christopher to be as challenging as we should have been? Any fears I had had about Angelina's changing her mind had been *before* birth, not after. It never occurred to me that she might change her mind after. It hadn't occurred to anyone. Well, possibly, to Neil.

Christopher and I watched while Neil assembled his gear on the kitchen counter like a true craftsman: a small round brush with a handle, a toothbrush with soft bristles, and a genuine chamois leather polishing cloth. The objects of his attention—black oxfords with laces removed—wore shoe trees. He buffed and shined first his shoes, then my boots, and we headed downtown to Family Court.

Wearing a navy blue suit, a white shirt, a red and blue striped tie, his sparkling black oxfords, and carrying a leather briefcase, Neil fully looked the part of a lawyer. He brought his own lawyer to court. Schwartz objected, of course, but Judge Finberg said a witness can "have somebody to protect whatever he thinks is necessary." Maybe he thought we were contemplating a malpractice suit against him, a proposal that my sister Katherine, an attorney, had made several months earlier when litigation began. Neil hadn't properly protected our interests, she said. But Jeremy and I felt we could get through only one legal proceeding at a time.

Norman led Neil through the now familiar set of questions. How had he met Angelina? What had she told him about adoption? Had Neil informed her of the alternatives? "Yes," Neil said, "but she said it wasn't the question of just financially supporting the child, and I asked her what she meant. She said it was a question of her having support, emotional support, for raising a child in the context of a family, and it was also a question of the child's needs in terms of being brought up in a family environment."

Norman proceeded by inquiring about Angelina's intent when she signed the placement-for-adoption document. Schwartz objected so frequently that Judge Finberg admonished him to save his arguments until the conclusion of the case.

Norman asked Neil whether there were any conditions placed on our taking Christopher from the hospital. "There was a discussion on circumcision," Neil replied. Schwartz leaned over to Norman and whispered, "Let's just cut this short." Norman grinned broadly. I was shocked that Schwartz would make such a crude joke in the midst of a serious proceeding. But then he and Norman were acting out their roles. They probably cared about us and Angelina, but we were clients. They had other clients, too.

Norman asked Neil, "Following Miss Rodriguez's discharge from the hospital, did you have any other conversation with her?"

"Two weeks after birth or so, approximately."

"What took place in that conversation?"

"It was late afternoon or early evening that I received a phone call from Angelina. She said, 'Mr. Hernandez.' I said, 'Yes.' She then said, 'How are you?' I said, 'Fine. How are you?' She said, 'I feel so sad and so empty.' I said, 'Oh. I am very sorry.' I think she might have repeated that and I think she started to cry or I felt that there was some choking in her voice. She said, 'It hurts. When will it stop hurting?' I said, 'Angelina, you realize that we did discuss this at our very first meeting.' Because at the very first meeting I had told her that it was foreseeable that she would have a feeling of regret or a feeling of loss and I had recommended at that time that maybe she might want to write down the reasons that she was placing the child for adoption. So that she could look back on it afterwards and remind herself of what she was thinking when she initiated the thing. So anyway—''

"Objection," said Schwartz. "Who initiated the thing?"

Overruled.

"In any case," continued Neil, "I said that we had discussed it, and feeling bad would be part of the thing, and then she said, 'Yes, but I didn't realize that it would be so painful.' And I said, 'Well, yes.' She wanted to know when she would stop feeling bad. I said, 'I can't tell you that.' Then she said, 'Well, I imagine that it would be very, very hard to get the child back. Do you think it would be possible?' At that point, I said, 'Angelina, I really can't talk to you about this. You have to talk to Mike Cole, and maybe you should speak to Father Ramo, but I can't answer any real questions because I do represent the Ryans. It would be complicated.' ''

"Excuse me?" said Schwartz.

"It would be complicated, and then she definitely had started to cry."

"Did you have any further conversations with her following that?" asked Norman.

"Yes, it would have been around two months later, in mid-October, I believe. I received a communication from her attorney, Mr. Posito. I had received a letter from Mike Cole informing me that he was no longer representing Angelina and that Mr. Posito was. On the basis of our telephone conversation, a meeting was arranged with Mr. Posito and Angelina in my office."

"And what took place at that meeting?"

"At that meeting I asked her if she really—if her request to get the baby back was absolutely final or would she be willing to reconsider it. I said to her that the Ryans were not eager to give up the child. That maybe she would like to think about it some more or avail herself of special counseling. I told her that Mrs. Ryan was willing to come to California to talk to her, and we basically discussed those things. As a result of the conversation, Angelina was going to think about the matter for another week or so and at the end of that week she would get back to Mr. Posito, who would get back to me to tell me what her ultimate decision was."

"I have no further questions, Judge," said Norman.

It was time to adjourn. Neil's attorney stepped forward to the bench. "Your Honor, may I just state that my client is here voluntarily. He has business commitments in the state of California, and if this proceeding is going to continue, I hope it continues tomorrow."

Judge Finberg said court would be closed the following day, which was Veterans Day. At our next court date three weeks later, the judge, Norman, and Schwartz held an extended discussion about the fact that the trial was dragging on. There had been two cancellations because of Schwartz's schedule; Norman had been ill, and Judge Finberg had been ill. Neil had returned to San Francisco for root canal surgery.

Schwartz said, "There is another reason why Mr. Hernandez is not here today, Judge. Upon examining his notes, I believe some of those notes were doctored."

"Just a minute, Counselor," said the judge. "I will not permit any such statement to be made about an attorney who is not before the Court. My impression of Mr. Hernandez is that he is a lawyer of a very high ethical standard.''

"Yes, that is correct," said Schwartz.

"As you recall," said the judge, "he testified that he consulted a priest. I don't mean to say that being a priest gives this person any particular status, but he did consult someone not of the legal profession and presumably with no kind of bias or interest in this case whatsoever. He asked the priest to recommend a lawyer who would be willing to serve the petitioner on a *pro bono* basis. He escorted the petitioner to this lawyer's office and left her there in the company of a lawyer who was not a person who had been known to Mr. Hernandez in any fashion before the priest had suggested his name. He left the petitioner at the lawyer's office with an interpreter. He also testified as to his various discussions with the petitioner of her options with regard to this child, and he also testified as to his referral of the petitioner to the hospital social worker.

"I realize he has not been cross-examined, and it may be that cross-examination will reveal some misrepresentation in this testimony. Assuming that it does not reveal any misrepresentation, Counselor, it is difficult for me to believe and I will not permit accusations of misconduct against this absent lawyer.''

"I'm not saying that at all," said Schwartz.

"You said—"

"That was Your Honor's conclusion.''

"You said that the notes were doctored.''

"Can I make my statement?" asked Schwartz. "It is very simple. I'm not testifying. I'm not making a statement as to what I didn't find. I am testifying as to what I did find, Judge, because in his reports he left out some billing sheets.''

"You used the term *doctored*. What do you mean?"

"There were no billing sheets before September, Your Honor. I presume that if a man accounts for every hour of his time, he should have billing sheets before that date."

"What is your conclusion from that?" asked the judge.

"My conclusion is that Miss Conroy, who pretended to be an objective witness, in fact—Mr. Hernandez would not even pick up telephone calls from her because on his own billing sheets it indicated that she began to curse him. She began to use profanities against him. He refused to accept phone calls."

Judge Finberg said, "I don't know what you are testifying about or purporting to testify about."

"I'm just saying, Your Honor, that these notes also reflect on the part of the Ryans a willingness also that they would stop at nothing to regain custody of this child. To keep custody." Schwartz's face was very red.

"I won't listen to any more of this," said the judge.

"I want those billing sheets," said Schwartz. "That's why he's not here today."

The colloquy continued, with Judge Finberg, Norman, and Schwartz arguing for several minutes about why court had been delayed for three weeks and why Neil wasn't present this particular day. The stenographer was told that the trial was going off the record while Norman tried to phone Neil in San Francisco about his next appearance. While waiting for Neil to return the call, Judge Finberg suggested that Norman call me as his next witness.

I was scared. I stated my name and marital status in a quavering voice. Watching the others on the witness stand simply hadn't prepared me for the fear I felt sitting in that chair. Norman had said to me earlier in the waiting area, "Be sure to cry. You saw how Finberg reacted when Eileen Conroy cried. Show some emotion up there."

"I don't know if I'll cry or not, Norman. I can't make myself cry."

"You're too statistical," said Norman. "You always remember this or that date, how many weeks, how many times. Just show some emotion."

That hurt. I sat brooding over Norman's comments while listening to the lawyers and the judge debate Neil's billing sheets. I couldn't figure out why Schwartz was rambling from one thing to another, what point he was trying to make.

"Statistical," Norman had called me. It sounded so flat, so boring. I had tried to reconstruct events of the past several months as carefully as possible for Norman, making an outline of people, dates, documents, comments, producing legal pads on which I'd recorded bits and pieces of conversations with Eileen, Neil, my gynecologist. It had become an editorial habit, an automatic reflex, useful to have. So I was statistical. Eileen was the type of witness a defense attorney would prefer, I supposed. More feminine, softer, giggly. Well, Norman was stuck with me, a statistical mother.

Norman asked me about my education. Schwartz said, "I'm going to object to any questions along that line."

"On what grounds?" asked the judge.

"On the grounds that it is not in issue," Schwartz replied.

"That leads me to a point that I was about to raise," said Judge Finberg. "Concerning the allegation that it would be in the best interest of the child to have custody awarded to the petitioner for the reason that she could provide a better home for the child. It is true that I don't believe that papers submitted to this Court include a specific request by the respondents for custody. Since the respondents presently have custody, and since the petitioner's petition puts custody in issue, if the petition were denied, custody would remain where it is. It is possible, however, that those seeking adoption do not wish custody of a child unless their adoption petition is granted. The Court addresses its question to the respondents' attorney. I think it might be well, Mr. Bernstein, for you to put in your papers whether your clients wish custody if their adoption petition is not granted. All right. Please go ahead with Mrs. Ryan."

Now what was all that about, I wondered. I *thought* the judge was recommending that we ask for custody in case we couldn't adopt, hinting that she would like to give us custody. My head was swimming as Norman resumed his questions. He asked me about my family, how I was introduced to Angelina and her situation. The letter I wrote to Mr. Arnaldo describing Jeremy and me and the home study that the Children's Aid Society had conducted in our home were accepted as exhibits.

When Norman asked me questions about Christopher's life with Jeremy and me, my responses were terse, laconic.

"What is Christopher's general health?"

"Excellent."

"Has he been treated by a physician on a regular basis?"

"Yes."

"And has he progressed normally as a child?"

"Yes. Flourished."

"Is Christopher walking at this time?"

"Yes."

"Does he speak?"

"Yes."

"What language does he speak?"

"English."

"Does he understand and respond to you when you talk to him?"

"Yes."

"Do you care for Christopher by yourself or do you have help to care for him?"

"I care for him by myself."

"Does Christopher have any peer relationships?"

"Yes, he has friends who come to our house and he goes to their houses."

I had been numbed by Norman's branding me as statistical; now I risked being a very boring witness. I should have painted a warm, harmonious family picture, with me bouncing Christopher on my hip while taking freshly baked bread from the oven as Daddy came home for dinner. At least I didn't mention my membership in a health club and the fact that Christopher went to a babysitter three mornings a week while I sweated through a calisthenics class, stretched on Nautilus machines, and swooned in the steam room.

Or worse, that I'd seen a therapist several times the previous spring. I had hoped that talking with a professional about my frustration and helplessness might be useful. It was the therapist who had recommended my joining the health club. "Do something for yourself," she'd advised.

I had held back from Carla at first. My Catholic background had taught me to view people who sought out psychiatric help as weak and indulgent. Then I'd warmed to her sympathetic approach, her probing, her interest in helping me. If only I could have answered Norman's questions as comfortably as I could answer Carla. Jeremy reluctantly agreed to go with me once to see Carla. At our next session alone, she told me I wasn't listening to him carefully enough.

After six or seven visits, I stopped seeing Carla. It was expensive; I had to pay a babysitter for Christopher; I wasn't sure we were getting anywhere. She seemed to feel that a resolution about Christopher would be necessary before I could really go on with my life.

Then Norman got down to the nitty-gritty.

"Did there come a time after the summer when you learned that Miss Rodriguez was reconsidering her decision to surrender the child?"

"Objection," said Schwartz, "that is leading. Mr. Hernandez testified that it came as early as August."

"I am asking *her*," said Norman.

Schwartz countered, "Let's just say when."

"Did there come a time when you learned that Miss Rodriguez was changing her mind regarding the adoption?"

"*Had* changed her mind, according to Mr. Hernandez, on August second," said Schwartz.

"Just a minute," said Judge Finberg. "Mr. Bernstein is asking the questions. If you find some inconsistencies between this testimony and Mr. Bernstein's testimony, you may point that out later."

"Yes," I replied. "It was in October."

I described the lunch with Saul Levine and our subsequent hiring of Norman as we prepared for litigation. The letter and Christmas card I wrote to Angelina, and her response, were entered as exhibits after an extended argument between Schwartz and Norman as to their relevance. Norman's final question to me was, "Mrs. Ryan, did you ever receive any petition or notice of a habeas corpus proceeding from the state of California?" I hadn't.

Judge Finberg announced a recess before cross-examination.

Angelina walked into the ladies room where I stood washing my hands at the sink. "It's cold today, yes?" I nodded as I walked out, too stunned to answer. I realized that aside from our initial exchange translated by Jorge Cabas, we had never spoken. It was more convenient for me to consider her simply as The Enemy, not as another woman with feelings. And if we were to speak, I'd never imagined we'd have a conversation about the weather. Maybe I thought she'd ask if she could see a photograph of Christopher, or how he was, or if he still took a bottle, or if he woke up during the night, or any of the hundreds of questions mothers of fifteen-month-olds exchange instinctively.

Schwartz began by attempts to discredit Eileen Conroy ("It is your testimony, then, that the only thing that you knew about her in connection with the adoption was that she had adopted a child herself?") and Neil Hernandez ("Did you ask Mr. Hernandez what other adoptions he had done when he was retained by yourself?").

"Yes," I said. "He told me that he had not done adoption work before. But he told me in approximately an hour and a half phone conversation of all the research that he had done to date, and I was impressed."

"In other words, he had already done work before he had even spoken to you on this case?"

"I believe that he had done research."

"Mr. Schwartz," said Judge Finberg, "what is the point of all this?"

"Your Honor, the question of who he represented—"

"There is no question that he did represent the Ryans," said the judge. "No question at all."

"Your Honor, let me put it this way to you. My offer of proof—"

"Perhaps it was not a very good idea to retain him, since he knew nothing about adoption," added Judge Finberg.

"Well," said Schwartz, "that was not the reason he

was retained. He was retained because he had an association with the employer of Miss Rodriguez. That is the fact."

"What does that have to do with it?" asked the judge.

"It has to do, Your Honor, with the coercive atmosphere that went on later that year after the child was born."

"Objection, Your Honor," said Norman. "There is no testimony as to any coercion at all."

Judge Finberg said, "No court is going to draw an inference of such a wild nature as you are suggesting, Mr. Schwartz. We are going to have to stop right now, anyway. It is five o'clock. That is all. The record is closed. We are going to continue on Thursday."

I could feel myself getting testy as Schwartz hammered away on Thursday. No chance for tears, just clear, cold anger at this man.

"Did you make up your mind that no matter what happened you would keep this child regardless of whether or not she signed the consent?"

"Yes."

"And at that time in October, the child was two and a half months old, correct?"

"I guess so."

"How old is the child now?"

"Almost seventeen months."

"And to date, did you get a consent in this case?"

"No."

"Did you know today that you cannot adopt a child without obtaining the consent signed before a judge in the state of California?"

"Look, I cannot make myself any clearer, Counsel," said Judge Finberg. "In my opinion, none of this cross-examination except for perhaps one or two questions is offering any illumination to the Court here at all. Mrs. Ryan is not a lawyer. The Court does not intend to be guided on the law by her opinion of it, Counsel. If Mr. Schwartz wants to spend the rest of the afternoon on these questions, I do not think that it is up to me to continually exhaust myself trying to explain why I believe they have no value to Counsel. But if Counsel thinks they are of value, it will have to be his judgment that will continue to control his activities. I realize that I could, of course, cut off the cross at any time on the basis of my view of it. However, I feel that in this case, which is a highly controversial one, it would be unwise for the Court to mandate that the cross-examination is over."

In his redirect examination following Schwartz's cross, Norman said to me, "You stated that you decided that you would not return the child to the mother. Tell the Court why not."

"He's our son."

"No further questions," said Norman.

Schwartz hopped up. "Do you know of any Court that recognizes that fact right now?"

"It's not for a Court to tell me," I said.

"No further questions."

A recess was called. I paced back and forth in front of Jeremy's chair in the waiting area. "I was terrible," I wailed. "I didn't say anything I had wanted to say. I didn't get a chance. Schwartz got me so mad."

"You were fine," Jeremy said, soothingly. "I liked it when you got feisty with him."

"I said it's not for a Court to tell me. How do you think Finberg liked that?"

"None of that matters; you heard her say that," Jeremy said.

"I didn't even cry. Norman must have been disappointed."

"Why give Schwartz the satisfaction of crying?" said Jeremy. He always had a rational answer, but I still felt like a colossal flop as a witness.

Later, when I related this incident to my sister, she said, "Remember Cordelia in *King Lear*? Her sisters raved on and on about their feelings for their father and they were lying. Cordelia said simply, 'He is my father.' The love is implicit."

I felt better but still spent several showers lathering my hair furiously with shampoo, reliving my moments on the stand and rewriting my testimony, "showing" Schwartz.

Back in the courtroom a few minutes later, Jeremy was called to the stand. I looked at him critically as he was sworn in, tried to see him through Judge Finberg's eyes. Actually, he could have passed for one of the lawyers we saw milling about the Family Court building. His single-breasted, gray, pinstriped suit fit his tall, slim frame well, gave him a look of authority.

Jeremy has beautiful hair. When we met, in the early seventies, it was long, reddish-brown, and curly. Now, in 1983, the curls had been clipped into waves and the brown was spiked with gray, particularly at the temples. Only his beard and mustache showed hints of red. The gray gives him a distinguished look, offset well by horn-rimmed glasses. He is a handsome man of whom one would say, "He has aged well."

Norman established that Jeremy came from a close-knit family, that he spent a lot of time with Christopher, and that we all went to church. Then he said, "You heard Maggie, your wife, testify that when she was asked through the various correspondents to return the child that she stated that she would not do so. Was this a decision she made on her own?"

"We decided together that we wanted to fight this and to keep the child," replied Jeremy.

"Why did you make that decision?"

"Because he is our son."

"What is your feeling toward him?"

"I love him and he loves us."

Schwartz began: "And this feeling, Mr. Ryan, about wanting to fight this, this feeling on your part began in August of 1982?"

"No."

"September of 1982?"

"No."

"October of 1982?"

"No."

"November 1982?"

"No."

"It started when the child was born?"

"No."

"When did it start?"

"July 9, 1983" (the date we first appeared before Judge Finberg).

"July 9, 1983?"

"Yes."

"Did you know that Miss Rodriguez wanted to have her child back as early as August 1982?"

"No. We were never told she wanted the child back. We had correspondence with her and she never asked for the child back. She wrote and inquired about the child but never once said that she wanted him back."

Schwartz asked Jeremy about custody. "Didn't you realize that as your own lawyers indicated to you in letters, you were considered to have only provisional custody?"

"We had custody."

"You felt that you had custody?"

"We did have custody."

"Permanent custody?"

"No, custody."

"Was the term *provisional custody* ever used to describe the legal relationship between you and your wife and this child?"

"I don't know what the term *provisional custody* means in terms of a legal relationship. We have custody."

"Was the term ever mentioned to you?"

"Not that I recall."

"In other words, you feel that the right to have custody of this child—"

"We do have custody."

"And you take no affirmative actions, is that what you feel?"

"Angelina signed a document giving us custody."

"When?"

"In July."

"In other words, because the child is physically in your custody, you feel that you have custody, sir?"

"I am saying we have custody."

"Do you consider it legal custody?"

"I don't know what the term *legal custody* means. We have custody."

"In other words, it was because *she* didn't say it to you, but said it to your attorney, that you think that you are in the right here?"

"We are all here to decide who is right," answered Jeremy.

Judge Finberg intervened. "I am not quite clear about your testimony myself, sir," she said to Jeremy. "Are you saying that you didn't fully realize that the petitioner was attempting to get her child? You didn't realize that until July 9 of this year, sir?"

Jeremy turned toward Judge Finberg, as if he were glad to have the opportunity to explain to her instead of to Schwartz. "No, I am saying that she never expressed that to us until July 9, which is the first time we met her. We had been told by other parties, third and fourth parties, that was the situation. We had correspondence with her during the period after October 1982 and prior to July 1983, wherein she didn't say that. We have handwritten notes from her. She did not ask for the child in those notes. All I am saying is—"

Judge Finberg nodded. "You are saying that although you did get such word from Mr. Hernandez that you didn't feel or you didn't take it as seriously as if you had heard it from her directly?"

"Directly or from a court or from somebody else," said Jeremy.

The judge scribbled on a legal pad, nodded to Schwartz, and said, "Proceed."

Schwartz ran a hand through his wiry hair. He looked tired and angry. "How many lawyers did you retain in this case?"

"One in California and two in New York."

"And despite the fact that you retained these lawyers, you didn't accept what they had to say to you?"

"What do you mean, I didn't accept it?" Jeremy asked.

"You just told us a moment ago that as far as you are concerned it would only be if Angelina related to you that she wanted custody that you would in fact have believed she did. Isn't that what you in effect said?"

"No," said Jeremy, calmly, slowly. "I am saying that I heard it third hand."

"Third hand? From whom, your lawyers?"

"Yes, my lawyers."

"And you didn't accept that."

"There was nothing to accept."

"And are you prepared to accept the ruling of this Court?"

"Yes."

"Would that be firsthand?"

"That is what the Court is here to decide, as I understand it."

"No further questions," said Schwartz. "I would now renew my longstanding request for visitation rights."

"You say longstanding," said Judge Finberg. "This is the first request, Counsel. I am going to deny the request. I hope that this proceeding will be terminated as expeditiously as possible, and certainly in the middle of this proceeding it would be an abuse of my discretion to direct visitation for a mother who has never seen her child. Adjourned to December sixteenth."

"Can we have the seventeenth?" requested Schwartz.

"December seventeenth. That's all," said the judge.

Nine

"You know, she's kind of cute," Saul Levine said, appraising Angelina in the Family Court waiting room the week before Christmas. "I wouldn't mind going out with her."

After questioning him on the stand about the legal research he had done in New York in tandem with Neil Hernandez in San Francisco, Norman asked Levine, "As a result of your observations of the Ryans, do you have an opinion of them as a married couple and as parents?"

Judge Finberg overruled Schwartz's objection.

"I think they are a loving couple, and they have a great deal of respect for each other as people."

"And what about their roles or relationship as parents?"

"I think they are intelligent parents in the sense that I happen to like children, and I observe how other people handle them, and I watch them. I think they have dealt with Christopher as intelligent human beings rather than gushy overbearing people."

"May I state my continuing objection to this?" interjected Schwartz.

"Maggie appears to be a very loving, caring mother; Jeremy in a much more masculine sense is also very tender and gentle and very loving toward their little boy."

Schwartz began his cross-examination by asking Levine, "Are you living with your wife at the present time?" (Later Levine told us he had chatted with Schwartz in the waiting area!)

"No, I'm not."

"And when you got married, did you have an opinion as to whether you could live with that woman for the rest of your days?"

"Yes, I did."

"Okay. Would you say you were wrong about that?"

"Today I would say I was wrong."

Because Levine testified that the bulk of his practice was marital law and he also testified to the strength of Jeremy's and my marriage, Schwartz was anxious to discredit Levine by illuminating his divorce.

Schwartz continued. "Do you recall receiving a letter from Mr. Hernandez in May of 1982 wherein there was an indication that Miss Rodriguez was beginning to show signs of reluctance?"

"I don't recall what was in the letter."

Judge Finberg said, "I think it would be much simpler to have the letter admitted in evidence."

"You see," said Schwartz, "I don't want to do that. That's why Mr. Hernandez's presence in New York would help me, but he got out after making direct testimony. He's not showing his face."

"He did not duck out," said Norman. "I object to that statement being on the record and ask that it be stricken."

"I'll withdraw that," said Schwartz. "He came for

direct examination and we can't get him for cross-examination."

"Don't worry about it," said the judge.

Levine was vague, as if he weren't sure about what had happened after he finished his legal research before Christopher's birth. Schwartz's questions were circuitous; Levine often answered, "I don't recall."

"Incidentally," said Schwartz, "was there any stipulation or condition with regard to the Ryans physically taking this child for adoption?"

"No."

"Well, do you recall that only a healthy child and not a child subject to a defect would be accepted by the Ryans?"

"Yes."

"And was that what you indicated to Mr. Hernandez?"

"Yes, I told them if the kid is sick, they should not take him out of the hospital."

"In other words, if the child was sick or subject to a defect, then the Ryans did not want the child?"

"No, that wasn't the issue. The issue was whether you take a sick child out of the hospital. In my opinion, being a parent, you don't take a sick kid out of the hospital."

"You're talking about a sick child in terms of a cold?"

"I'm talking about a sick child. I don't care if you call it a sick child if he's got a cold or he's missing a foot. If he needs to be in the hospital, the kid stays in the hospital. That's all."

"Do you recall," said Schwartz, "Mr. Hernandez writing to you with regard to the specifics of the agreement? Last paragraph, first page: 'I understand that the Ryans will accept any issue of Miss Rodriguez provided, however, that the child is not born with such a defect or condition as would require institutionalization or continual medical and therapeutic treatment or care.' "

"That's what he said."

"Do you know why he would write this understanding of the Ryans to you?"

"No. I told them that it was something that I didn't think that they ought to even worry about, because it's very, very rare. The second thing I told them was that if you have a beautiful child, and he's born with an arm missing, so what? And they agreed with me."

"They agreed with you?"

"Yes."

"Did you write any letter to Mr. Hernandez correcting this misstatement or supposition that was supposedly, to you, erroneous?"

"I don't recall writing him any letters."

"Nothing further, Your Honor."

Norman said, "When are we going to see Mr. Hernandez in person? Do we have an update on his dental condition?"

"I don't know," said Judge Finberg. "Do you insist on having all of this on the record or can we excuse the reporter? Good-bye."

Norman's gaze wandered around the crowded living room at our Christmas party. "Don't you have any married girlfriends with kids?" he asked. "We need a mother to testify for you." I scanned the guests. There was Elaine, my confidante, divorced, seriously involved with Bill, but single and childless at the moment. Ellen and Jane, gay. Katy and Tom, career-minded, no desire for children. Patrick and Glen, priests.

"I know that woman," Norman said excitedly, pointing at Jeremy's partner's sister-in-law, visiting from Atlanta for the holiday. "Is she married? Kids?" Norman and Connie were soon deep in conversation; they had gone to high school together in Queens. Connie's two children, aged about four and six, and Christopher were in a high state of excitement, touching the white lights on the shimmering Christmas tree, then jumping back, shrieking, as if they'd been burned. Chris and Jeremy wore matching rust-colored Shetland crewnecks with muted stripes knitted into the arms, my early Christmas gift. At seventeen months, Christopher was just beginning to talk, and he kept up a steady stream of observations, notably, "Yights, yights, yook, Mommy, yights," pointing with wonder at the small white tree lights.

"She won't do it," said Norman. "Too busy with the relatives." I couldn't really blame Connie for not wanting to testify for us. She didn't know Jeremy and me well, and her brother-in-law's partner's custody problems weren't her concern.

We'd been assigned court dates on December 22 and 23, but Neil wasn't willing to come back to New York to testify during Christmas week. We arranged for Christopher's pediatrician, a dignified, sixtyish, serious gentleman who served as attending pediatrician at the New York Foundling Hospital as well as conducting his own practice to testify. Also testifying on the same afternoon was the Executive Director of the Children's Aid Society, a business colleague of Jeremy's. In the past he had supervised placement of over five hundred children for adoption.

Norman suggested that his brother Lester, also an attorney, examine these witnesses. I found this midstream switch frightening, but Norman assured us that "it wasn't a big deal." He'd told Lester everything.

Lester must have been a couple of years younger than Norman. His chocolate brown shirt stood out amidst the sea of white-shirted lawyers. He chewed gum.

Schwartz became increasingly testy as it came clear that Lester intended to qualify the pediatrician and the Children's Aid Society executive as expert witnesses, enabling them to comment on hypothetical ramifications of Christopher's future with Angelina because of their vast experience.

"He's trying to apply the Children's Aid Society guidelines when they have nothing to do with this case," complained Schwartz, pointing at Lester.

"Mr. Schwartz," said Judge Finberg, "I don't believe that your views are—"

"Your Honor, I think I know *where* my views stand in this Court."

The judge removed her glasses. "Excuse me," she said to Schwartz in a stern tone. "What does that remark mean?"

"What does that remark mean that I just addressed to the Court?"

"Yes."

"Nothing, Your Honor," Schwartz said innocently.

"I would like you to apologize."

"I certainly do, Your Honor." Schwartz's voice was respectful, genuinely surprised.

"Please do not ever make any comments about this Court's conduct unless you are willing to support them or to be held in contempt."

"Fine," said Schwartz.

The Children's Aid executive testified to both a business and social relationship with Jeremy and me. He said that we met the standard of good qualifications for adoptive parents, "people who are emotionally stable, who are mature, who have had life experiences in which there has been love so that they in turn can love others and can provide security. People who are not explosive or impatient. People who can nurture a child and provide a loving kind of secure home for a child." In his opinion, transferring Christopher from us to Angelina would be a "change that would be very detrimental."

The pediatrician stated that to remove a child suddenly

"from a home which he has been brought up in and has known, has loved his family, can cause in that child a certain amount of repression, of nightmares, of behavior disorder, of eating problems, of fear in terms of relationships to other adults."

Schwartz approached both of these witnesses in the same manner; that is, he attempted to secure their agreement that Jeremy and I exacerbated the situation by stonewalling. He said to Christopher's pediatrician, "So you think the respective adoptive parents acted in the best interest of the child realizing they had a child which was never really legally given to them?"

"That is not a fact in evidence at all," said Judge Finberg.

"It certainly is, Your Honor," maintained Schwartz.

"I don't wish to debate it with you, Mr. Schwartz. That is *not* a fact in evidence."

"Do you think it would be in the best interest of the child to resolve the situation with regard to custody and adoption early in the child's life?" asked Schwartz.

"I can't answer," replied Dr. Burns.

"Do you think it's better to wait as the child grows older?" persisted Schwartz.

"I think it depends on the child and the people involved," said the doctor evenly. "I think it is easier and to the child's advantage to be in one place, period, rather than spend a long period of time in one area then go to another area."

I'm not certain I'd seen Patrick in his white collar and clerical black shirt and trousers before, but I was grateful that he'd worn them for his court appearance the next afternoon.

Patrick was barely thirty, young for an assistant pastor. Our church had been his first assignment after the seminary. He told the Court: "The image I had when I first met them, those first several months, was of Maggie with Christopher in one of those little holders kind of strapped around her shoulders." Lester interjected, "Indicating on the chest of the body, if it pleases the Court."

Lester concluded his direct examination by asking Patrick, "Father, have you formed an opinion as to whether or not it would be in the best interest of this child *spiritually* for him to be removed from the Ryans and to be given to the natural mother?" Schwartz's objection was sustained.

Schwartz asked Patrick, "If you felt that some weeks after the child was born, the Ryans ignored the problem that the natural mother had not in reality signed the proper consent to give up the child—" He paused, then said, dramatically, "*Morally*, wouldn't that be the time to resolve the issue one way or another? Do you think waiting a year and a half would be more proper in terms of a moral outlook—"

"Objection," said Lester. "This assumes the Ryans ignored something that is not in evidence whatsoever."

Judge Finberg said, "The fact is not established in the record in the Court's opinion that the Ryans knew the documents were insufficient, and the objection is sustained."

"May I state for the record that the Ryans took the stand and they admitted—" countered Schwartz.

"Can't you ask a simple question?" said the judge. "May I, please?" She turned toward Patrick. "If persons who are not the biological parents of a child but who wish to adopt a child are aware that all of the legal requirements needed for the child's adoption have not been satisfied, would you consider it morally important that they attempt to make their right to adopt the child certain or their lack of right to adopt the child certain as soon as possible?"

"I'll go along with the question," said Schwartz magnanimously.

Patrick answered, "I would say there would be a responsibility on the part of the persons involved to try to resolve the situation one way or the other."

We had decided to stay home for Christmas. Often we'd travel to my family in Chicago or Jeremy's parents in St. Louis, but this year I was singing in the church choir at midnight Mass on Christmas Eve. I'd started going to church again just after Christopher was baptized.

Actually, Christopher was baptized twice. The first occasion was at home, when he was twelve days old, and a United Church of Christ minister (a friend of my brother-in-law) performed the ceremony. Our motive for having him baptized in a church six months later was to procure a baptismal certificate. We had no documents bearing Chris's name. I walked around the block to the Catholic church one snowy January morning carrying Christopher in the Snugli.

A bearded young man wearing jeans and a plaid woolen shirt greeted us warmly. "Are you a priest?" I asked suspiciously.

Patrick Reilly, O.F.M., asked me why we wanted Christopher baptized. I replied that we wanted him to enter into the community of Christians. Patrick asked me whether I believed in original sin. I had been raised a Catholic and was taught that because of the sin of Adam and Eve in the Garden of Eden, we are all born with the stain of original sin on our souls. Feeling brave, I said I couldn't buy the theory that an innocent baby could have sinned. Patrick agreed with me. (I later discovered that the church had made extraordinary advances since my defection. As a result of the Second Vatican Council in the mid-1960s, the emphasis on original sin in the sacrament of baptism had been clarified to mean the situation of the world into which we are born, not any inherent evil in the person being baptized.)

Christopher was baptized the following Saturday afternoon in the dark, beautiful, cavernous old church. Fr. Patrick, my mother (visiting us for a month and delighted to serve as proxy for my sister and brother-in-law in Miami), Jeremy, Christopher, and I hovered around the stone baptismal font near the altar, lit by powerful overhead lights while the rest of the church remained in darkness, punctuated only by flickering votive candles in the rear and a violet streak from a stained-glass window. Patrick lit a special baptismal candle for Christopher and suggested that we light it every year on the anniversary of the baptism. We all sang along weakly to a tape of "Come to the Water." Then Patrick poured a few drops of water on Chris's thick head of hair and baptized him in the name of the Father, the Son, and the Holy Ghost. Afterward, Patrick came to our house for cheese, pâté, French bread, and champagne.

This elitist approach to Christopher's entry into the Christian community became the springboard for my own return to the church. My mother and I attended Mass the next morning. The homily was inspiring, the prayer comforting, the singing and guitar playing soothing. I continued to attend Mass on Sundays from then on. The language was simpler than I had remembered; the approach, cleaner; the experience, demystified. Peace and serenity worked on me like a sedative, calming me, assuaging my fears. My problem was tears; I dissolved constantly. When I came home to Jeremy and Christopher, I felt energized yet controlled.

When Christopher began to walk, he accompanied me

to Mass. Slowly we began to make friends at church, some of them children. Brother Martin, the elderly Italian sacristan, took a particular liking to Chris. We often walked around the block mid-week so Christopher could climb up and down the stone steps outside the church. Brother Martin enjoyed playing hide-and-seek with Christopher behind the pillars.

Patrick had become a friend, a confidant. Every Sunday after Mass I brought him up to date on the most recent developments in our struggle.

On Christmas Eve, we had a dinner party for a friend and most of her family from Chicago, who were spending the holiday in the city. I'd known Peggy since first grade, and I imagine we'll always be friends. Since her father had died a few years before, her mother prefers spending Christmas in New York, with her married daughter. During dinner, Peggy and her three sisters and her mother sided against her younger brother, Tom, who at twenty-six was balking at having braces put on his teeth. He taught eighth grade and imagined his students jeering him out of the classroom. Most of his family thought he should suffer through the two years of braces and not be so vain. Peggy apologized for the banal conversation, but I was complimented that her family was comfortable enough to discuss such typical family fare in our presence.

It was difficult to pull myself away from the party to arrive at church in time for the caroling before Mass. The night was bitter cold, but I felt warm from the wine with dinner and the cognac with dessert. As I climbed the winding stairs to the choir loft, a glow infused me. Probably much of it came from the alcohol, but it *had* been a euphoric evening. Knowing that Christopher was safely tucked into his crib and that Jeremy was graciously regaling our guests until a few of them wandered over to church, I felt content, filled. It was especially moving now to hear the traditional first reading at midnight mass:

> For unto us a Child is born
> Unto us a Son is given

We were invited upstairs to our neighbors, the Wittmans, for Christmas dinner the next day. Theo Wittman and I were becoming friends. She was a slim, intense Italian woman in her early forties, with thick, copper curls that seemed to spring from her head.

Theo had invited a mixed group of people. The dinner was stylized, elaborate. Mousse pâté with truffles and champagne before dinner. Roast goose stuffed with chestnuts. Marzipan. Christopher eschewed this rich array; I had to sneak downstairs to our loft and grill him a cheese sandwich.

After dinner, one of the guests treated us to a violin solo. Christopher sat curled on my lap, his mop of black curls stark against his white turtleneck.

A week later we were in Chicago for my sister Katherine's wedding. The airline lost Christopher's suitcase for several days. As I shopped for overalls, I wondered what size to buy. Size 2, which would fit now, or size 3, which would also fit next year? As always, in the back of my mind, was the thought: Will Christopher be with us next year? The thought unnerved me; I bought two pairs of size 3 overalls and one pair of size 4.

Neil Hernandez returned to New York in mid-January for Schwartz's cross-examination. He hadn't had the root canal—a scheduling problem, or it hadn't been necessary; the explanation was unclear. Neil's second visit was easier for us because we knew what to expect. He spent time with friends in New York. He was delighted to discover that the Nautilus Club around the corner from us honored his San Francisco membership. He seemed an unlikely sort for working out, with his slight physique and somewhat intellectual bent, but apparently he was a regular in San Francisco.

As Neil and I walked up the steps at the Lafayette Street subway stop, we ran into Schwartz. He and Neil smiled at each other and shook hands. "I've just come from a conference with my son's first grade teacher," said Schwartz. "She says he thinks school is for play. He has to start working." He shook his head as if his son were quite the character. "You might look into the school," he said to me. "It's a really good one." That's odd, I thought. Schwartz recommending a school for Christopher three years from now? Does he think we might win?

In the courtroom, Schwartz began by attempting to discredit any help Neil might have been to Angelina. "The first efforts to help her in terms of counseling, getting her counsel of her own, all took place after she signed the document which purportedly gave up custody and allowed the Ryans to take possession of her son?"

"How you interpret that document is for the Court, but that was after she signed the declaration of intent to place the child," said Neil.

"Did you know at the time that she was making, what, eighty dollars a week?"

"Around that, yes," replied Neil.

"Did you know she was in this country illegally?"

"I suspected it."

"Mr. Arnaldo, the lawyer who employed her, didn't tell you that she was here illegally?"

"No, he did not."

"Eileen Conroy didn't tell you she was here illegally?"

"No, she did not."

"Had you known for certain that she was here illegally,

would that change in any manner the approach that you took to the case?"

"Just a minute," said the judge. "I think I have to exercise the judge's duty of not permitting this cross-examination to go all over the tangential and irrelevant field."

"And you knew, I presume, she didn't speak English on or about April 30, 1982?"

"That's correct."

"So you suspected that she was illegally in this country? You knew she made approximately eighty dollars a week? You knew she didn't speak English? She was working for an associate of yours."

"Please don't sum up," said Judge Finberg.

"I'm going to ask a question," said Schwartz. "You did not, knowing all these things, advise her to seek any sort of counseling before she signed the document on April 30, 1982?"

"That's right," said Neil.

Then Schwartz rehashed whether or not Neil had informed Angelina about various agencies she might seek out for aid. He questioned Neil about Angelina's *pro bono* attorney. They discussed the documents signed, the court date scheduled for final consent, the judge's unavailability, over and over again.

Schwartz asked Neil, "According to the general outline you explained to Miss Rodriguez, did she follow the legal ramifications of this procedure?"

Neil said, "I can't tell you exactly how much she assimilated or how much she was able to understand the California statutory proceeding in adoption cases. I explained to her the best I could. When she said to me, 'Would it be possible to get the baby back? I imagine it would be very difficult,' that indicated to me that certainly she felt that the whole thing was final and irrevocable."

Schwartz said, "And if in fact she took the course not to appear before a superior court judge and not to cooperate and not to do the things that were supposed to be done if one was going to go ahead with it—"

"I'm going to draw a halt to this," said the judge. "I'm not going to permit you to go over it a fifth time."

"Wasn't it a fact," said Schwartz, "that the intent of having Mr. Cole withdraw from representing Miss Rodriguez and having you, Mr. Hernandez, withdraw from representing Mr. and Mrs. Ryan was so that it would become geographically and financially virtually impossible for Miss Rodriguez to proceed owing to her own financial ability at that time?"

"No," said Neil firmly, "Mr. Cole and I did not collude."

"Now in May," said Schwartz, "was there some reason for you to believe she might change her mind?"

"In May or June," said Neil, "it was Angelina herself who gave me a call, told me she had been given a baby shower and she had been told by the people she was living with that if she put the child up for adoption, it would indicate that she had a black heart."

"You have any notes there?" said Schwartz.

"She said, 'Do you think I would have a black heart for doing this?' It was at this point that I advised her to speak to a priest, and she did, and then came back to tell me she was feeling much better and wanted to go through with this."

Judge Finberg said, "It's now almost five o'clock. Is there some offer of proof you can make, Mr. Schwartz? We're going to conclude in the next five minutes."

"I don't see any reason why we shouldn't be able to, Judge," said Schwartz pleasantly. And he proceeded to present the business about our qualifying that we wanted to take only a healthy child. "If the child was—had a problem, for example, was institutionalized, then that child was to be Miss Rodriguez's child and not the Ryans' child. They wouldn't take that child."

"Objection," said Norman.

"Sustained," said Judge Finberg. "We're going to adjourn now."

Norman was allowed a brief redirect and established the fact that it was Neil's intent that Angelina execute the placement-for-adoption document to consent to the placement of Christopher for adoption.

"And only when the consent was *signed* would the adoption take place," chimed in Schwartz.

"We all understand that point," said Judge Finberg. "It's not necessary to keep repeating it. All right, Mr. Hernandez is excused. Have a good trip back to California." She smiled at Neil. "Do we have a witness scheduled for tomorrow?" she asked Norman.

"Yes," he answered. "We have Dr. Krinski, who is a child psychiatrist."

Ten

It had been Norman's suggestion that we bring in the testimony of a child psychiatrist to support our best interests of the child's position. "I must confess straight away that I have a prejudice in this case," Dr. Krinski said after I'd given him a brief outline of our situation over the telephone. His cool, clipped accent was probably English.

"What kind?" I asked warily.

"For you, the adoptive parents."

"Oh, good." I laughed nervously with relief. I'd assumed he meant a prejudice for Angelina.

As I changed Christopher's diapers in Gregory Krinski's waiting room, I prayed that Chris would make a good impression. He was rather shy, particularly with new acquaintances, and I hoped he wouldn't appear clingy or uncooperative.

Jeremy, Christopher, and I watched in silence as Dr. Krinski set up a large, soft rubber Mommy and Daddy, dressed as housewife and businessman à la 1950, and a nude baby on the floor several feet away from our chairs.

Then the doctor sat down on the far side of the room. After entwining himself around my knee for a while, Chris's curiosity got the better of him and he ambled over toward the trio of dolls. He seemed to sense that he was supposed to perform for us. Stuffing his hands in his overall pockets, he gazed down at the dolls, then walked around them with a studied nonchalance. As he bent down to pick up the baby, he knocked the mother doll over. I looked quickly at Dr. Krinski to see his reaction. He smiled and said he'd like to talk with Jeremy and me while continuing to observe Christopher's behavior. He asked us the now familiar lines of questions: When had we met? How long had we been married? Any history of alcohol or drug abuse? How large were our extended families? How did we become involved with Christopher?

Jeremy answered in his usual confident manner, straightforward, earnest, considering each question seriously before responding. I began to relax, particularly when describing Chris's behavior, routine, friends. Christopher had drifted away from the dolls and was tugging at the cord that lowered the Venetian blinds. "Chris—" I began, but Dr. Krinski said, "He's fine, let him be."

We were in the doctor's office almost ninety minutes. Christopher was very good, wandering back and forth from Jeremy to me, climbing on us, snacking on a rice cake, going back for a closer look at the dolls, trying the door handle. "Originally I planned to see you all again separately and to meet the biological mother," said Dr. Krinski, "but I don't think it's necessary. Christopher most certainly belongs with you." Dr. Krinski agreed to testify for us.

Lester Bernstein took Norman's place again as our attorney. After establishing Dr. Krinski's credentials, Lester said, "Doctor, are you familiar with something called the attachment theory?"

"Yes."

"Could you explain to the Court briefly what the attachment theory is?"

"The attachment theory holds that in order for positive psychological development to occur for an infant, an attachment must be formed between the infant and the adult, the caretaker, the parenting figure. Once this secure attachment is formed, which is called bonding, positive development of the child can occur. This attachment is an essential prerequisite."

"And in the case of the Ryans and Christopher, have you formed an opinion as to whether that bonding has positively formed?"

"Yes, there is a bonding, an attachment."

"And is there an apparent result if there is an interruption of this bonding, from a medical standpoint, a psychiatric standpoint?"

Schwartz objected.

"Do you mean in theory or in fact with this child?" asked Judge Finberg. Lester answered in theory and Schwartz was overruled.

"Well," said Dr. Krinski, "once a bond has been formed, if the child is separated from the people with whom the bond has been formed, the child becomes vulnerable and adrift to several possible detrimental consequences. They range from short-term consequences of acute distress to long-term consequences of perhaps ongoing depression for the child in later life when he becomes an adult. They can take the form of a serious interruption in the capacity to form important relationships with other human beings in the future. There is some evidence that delinquent behavior and a generally non-trusting approach to life can result."

"Christopher is approximately nineteen months of age," said Lester. "He has been in the custody of the

Ryans since his birth. His biological mother is a non-English-speaking alien who seeks to gain custody. In your opinion, what would the effect on Christopher be, from a psychiatric standpoint, if custody were removed from the Ryans and given to Miss Rodriguez?"

Objection overruled.

"I think that the results cannot, in any way that I can conceive of, be positive. If he were extremely fortunate, they might be neutral, but more likely they will be negative for Christopher. Nothing good can happen from it and a lot of bad things can happen from it."

"When you say nothing good can happen, would you please explain what you mean by that, Doctor?" requested Lester.

"It is beyond my realm of conception how it can in any way be good to remove a normally developing healthy child from a loving home where he is securely growing up. I cannot see how interrupting that could lead to anything good."

Schwartz began his cross-examination by asking Dr. Krinski if he thought the bonding would have already taken place when Angelina began requesting Christopher two or three months after birth.

"Mr. Schwartz, let's not play games about this," said Judge Finberg. "It is obvious where your questions are leading. I don't think it is up to this witness to pass on what fault lies with the Ryans in not having seen that this child was returned at that time. I simply will not spend another afternoon listening to that all over again."

"I've been at cross-examination for two minutes and Your Honor is limiting me," Schwartz said angrily.

"I am and I think it is justifiable. Whether you are here for one minute or twenty minutes, I nevertheless am going to perform the proper role for a trial judge, which is to limit cross-examination."

Schwartz sighed. "Would your opinion of the Ryans be affected by the fact that before they had final custody, they refused to turn over the child to the natural mother—"

"Objection," said Lester quickly.

"Sustained," said the judge. "This witness was not appraising the Ryans on the basis of the merit or demerit of their moves in litigation, and I am simply not going to permit this to be a farce."

"Let me just say to the Court—" began Schwartz.

"You have heard my ruling, Mr. Schwartz," said Judge Finberg. "Do you want to proceed to something which is illuminating?"

"If there were some problems with this child," Schwartz asked Dr. Krinski, "couldn't child therapy treat them?"

"One doesn't cause an illness in order to prove that it can be treated," said the psychiatrist.

"You can't get over the illness through child therapy?" persisted Schwartz.

"It is not inevitable," said Dr. Krinski evenly.

"But there is a possibility that this child could be perfectly normal without therapy?"

"There is that possibility."

"If separated from the Ryans?"

"Yes."

"And I presume that result would have a better chance of occurring had the separation occurred earlier?"

"The child would have a better chance of not being severly impaired if the separation occurred earlier," said the doctor.

Schwartz looked pleased. He continued, "In your experience as a psychiatric pediatrician, have you seen any detrimental consequences involving adoptive parents?"

"It depends to a large extent on what age the child is adopted at."

"Let's talk about this case," Schwartz directed.

"I think there is little doubt if the child learns that he is adopted, if this is openly handled, and if he lives in a warm and loving family environment, the detrimental consequences are likely to be minimal and probably nonexistent."

"Do you agree there would be some benefits for a child to be with his natural mother?" asked Schwartz.

"As distinguished—"

"As opposed to adoptive parents."

Judge Finberg interjected, "Would you say that an adoptive child may evidence some degree of conflict about his or her adoption?"

"Yes," said Dr. Krinski.

"And to what extent or how does such a conflict manifest itself?" asked the judge.

"I think this is very much related to the age of the adoption. If the adoption occurred early, if there had not been the process of a psychological attachment to another person, the conflict is transient, it presents no major problem."

Schwartz said, "If a child later on in life, when it was intellectually able to understand—converse with the parents—learned that his mother two months after his birth had requested that he be given back to her and the prospective parents refused to do that, do you think that might have detrimental effects on the psychological makeup of the child?"

"You understand that I have to give you a highly speculative answer," said Dr. Krinski. "My speculative answer is again, other things being equal, that the child's reaction would be a combination of a heightened sense of security in the love of his parents and sadness at the fact that he has never seen his biological mother."

"Do you think he may have some feeling of abandonment from his mother?"

"His parents didn't abandon him; they are the parents."

"The biological mother?" queried Schwartz.

"I am talking about the parents from the perspective of the child," answered Dr. Krinski.

"Would the child suffer any detriment as a result of knowing that his natural mother had abandoned him for a two-month period?"

"He would feel sad about it," said the doctor.

"Have you heard of the situation, Doctor, in your studies, where children were overjoyed to go back to their natural parents?"

"Objection." Lester was on his feet.

"If the biological mother now appears in the child's life, she will be conceived of as a stranger. There is no tie to her. The child's reaction of stress would be separation from what he conceives of as his natural parents."

"Have there been situations where the child got to love his biological parents?"

"Yes."

"And, Doctor, are there situations where that had occurred to the detriment of the prospective adoptive parents?"

"I am assuming that a child can learn to love any adult that he goes to live with. That is not the issue here. The issue is the price the child pays prior to—"

Schwartz cut him off. "But your testimony, your research studies indicate there is a possibility that there might not be a detrimental result; there might be a neutral result?"

"Neutral at best, but there are so many variables . . ."

"Do you have any perception in this case whether or not this particular child would be a delinquent if he goes back to his natural mother?"

"I can't tell that."

"Or would suffer from depression in this case? Do you have any evidence of that?"

"No."

"Or any evidence that this particular child would have difficulty in forming a relationship in the future?"

"No, I don't have any evidence of that. I do have evidence that this child is securely attached in a positive home."

"But there is no evidence that this child at this point would suffer any detrimental consequences?"

"That is right."

"No further questions," said Schwartz.

Lester began his redirect. "Doctor, during the course of your consultation with the Ryans, was adoption of Christopher discussed openly in front of you?"

"Certainly."

"How would you characterize the relationship between the Ryans and the child in respect to the subject of adoption?"

"It is irrelevant at this age," said Dr. Krinski. "A child at the age of nineteen months doesn't have a concept, cannot conceive of adoption. But the way they handle their openness in dealing with the issue gives me very good feelings about the way they will handle it once it becomes an issue for the child."

We had presented our case, calling on the testimony of our two attorneys, our liaison with Angelina (Eileen Conroy), the California hospital social worker (Pat Henderson), our parish priest, Christopher's pediatrician, a child psychiatrist, a family therapist, the Children's Aid

Society executive director and one of their social workers, Jeremy's friend Mark, and Jeremy and me. Schwartz had produced Angelina. Because she didn't have the "financial resources of the other side," he said, it would not be possible for her to call in any California witnesses. But he did intend to recall her to the stand.

At our next court date, an attractive, well-dressed woman in her mid-thirties stood chatting with Schwartz and Angelina by the windows. "Find out who she is," I said to Norman. "Maybe it's Angelina's English teacher?" I speculated to Jeremy. It was Angelina's current employer, the owner of a Fifth Avenue duplex penthouse. Maya Lieberman carried her mink coat with her to the stand, resting it carefully on the witness chair as she was sworn in, then draping it over her lap when she sat down.

When asked by Schwartz what language she spoke to Angelina, Mrs. Lieberman answered, "American."

"Basically there wasn't really any period of adjustment when she came to us," Mrs. Lieberman testified. "She seemed to adjust, fit into the family very nicely. We felt very comfortable with her and I think she did with us also." Angelina's salary was $120 for ten to twelve hours of work, five days a week. "She helps me with the children and with household work."

"Have you had an opportunity to observe Miss Rodriguez with your own children?" asked Schwartz.

"Yes," nodded Mrs. Lieberman. "I am around quite a bit, and I have seen her with both my children and especially my little daughter, who is eight. They relate to each other. Angelina has been trying to teach her some Spanish. Angelina has been reading to her and playing different games. I often leave her alone with Angelina, and there have never been any problems."

Schwartz concluded his questions with, "Incidentally, has anybody told you she might be an illegal alien?"

The answer was, of course, "No."

Schwartz recalled Angelina for rebuttal. When she had originally testified the previous fall, there had been no discussion of Angelina's plan for the future if she were to get custody of Christopher. Now she said, "I told my mother that I had fallen in love. That I had a son. I was afraid to tell her, but she is my mother and she has the right to know everything that happens to me."

"What did she say?" asked Schwartz.

"She immediately said, 'Daughter, come home. This is your home. Don't worry because we will help you.' I told her that because I was here alone in the United States I had given the son for adoption. He was now with another family. I told her I was fighting the case. She said, 'Well, dear, I am praying to God.' I told her if I won the case I would go to El Salvador."

Norman began his cross-examination by asking Angelina, "Are you aware of the current conditions in El Salvador regarding the guerrilla warfare going on there?"

"Yes."

"And is this warfare taking place near the city where your family lives?"

"There have been encounters," said Angelina.

Angelina hadn't contacted her brothers and sisters. Judge Finberg said, "You have attempted, Mr. Schwartz, to establish that the best interest of your witness's child would be served because various brothers and sisters were going to help her take care of this child. We still haven't seen any communication from anyone indicating any intention of anyone to help her."

The interpreter broke in to say, "The witness would like to offer an alternative plan."

"What is that?" asked the judge.

"A plan that the father of my child's sister has told me to come to their house," said Angelina. "They are going to help me. The child's father will help in California."

"Under what conditions would you use this alternate plan?" asked Judge Finberg.

"Well, I would feel fine there in the family. It wouldn't cost me anything," said Angelina.

"I am asking you," said Judge Finberg firmly, "under what circumstances would you choose that alternative plan to go to California?"

"Well, because of the guerrillas in Salvador. It is bad there and I want to have protection for Lorenzo." Then Angelina added, "I would marry Perez and we would live together. Sunday we spoke and he told me that he was willing for us to get married."

Two weeks later Christopher's biological father was in Family Court to testify. Antonio Rafael Perez was short. His build was stocky. He walked with a bit of a swagger. His face was round and smooth, babyish, but his hairline receded, leaving an exposed, high forehead. He wore a bright pink shirt with a spread collar under a navy blue sport jacket. A gold chain hung around his neck. He had brought a friend with him to court, another short Hispanic male, and the two man and Angelina sat silently in a row in the waiting area until Schwartz arrived. It occurred to Jeremy that Perez might be a ringer. I remembered what Neil had told us, that Perez had lost the ends of four fingers to a grenade in combat, and asked Norman to wander over to talk with Schwartz and check out Perez's right hand. Norman confirmed that Perez was Perez.

In spite of his cocky demeanor in the waiting area,

Perez appeared cowed by the courtroom. He never met anyone's eyes when he testified.

Schwartz established that Perez earned $9.04 an hour as a janitor, that he had met Angelina when she began renting a room from his sister, and that he and Angelina would return to El Salvador "if the situation is fixed."

In his cross-examination, Norman asked Perez, "From September of 1982 until three weeks ago, you never discussed marriage at all with Miss Rodriguez?"

"No, because I couldn't find her. She would hide from me always. She did evade me. She would tell my sister she didn't want to see me."

"After you terminated your relationship with Angelina, did you have relationships with other women?" asked Norman.

"That is not necessary for me to say," Perez replied, looking down.

"You are instructed to answer," said Judge Finberg.

"Yes."

"Are you going to plan to get married whether or not Angelina is successful in regaining the custody of your son?"

"Yes."

"Mr. Perez, when was the last time you had a relationship with another woman?"

"Yesterday."

"No further questions, Judge," said Norman.

Angelina stared straight ahead, impassive, inscrutable.

"I would like to ask the witness a question," said Judge Finberg. "Mr. Perez, do you have other children that you know of?"

"No."

"That is, in El Salvador?"

"No."

"Or in San Francisco?"

"No."

"Or anyplace else?"

"No."

"Are you sure of that?"

"Yes."

"No woman has ever told you that you had impregnated her other than Miss Rodriguez?"

"I am going to object to that question," said Schwartz.

"All right," said the judge, "is that all with this witness?"

"Yes," said Norman.

"Do you rest, Mr. Schwartz?" asked the judge.

"Yes."

"Mr. Bernstein?"

"I will notify the Court by Thursday morning as to whether I will need any other witnesses," said Norman.

Jeremy and I shared an elevator with Perez and Angelina for the eight flights to the ground floor. As Jeremy, who is six foot three, glared at him, Perez, who is probably five foot six, moved backward to the corner and appeared to shrink. Angelina tossed her head and stared at the elevator door. The trial was over.

CHAPTER
Eleven

Snow of any magnitude is unusual in New York City. Seven inches of snow in April is absolutely bizarre. On April 16, Christopher and I borrowed my neighbor's Flexible Flyer and ventured out on to the powdered sidewalks of Soho. As we headed toward West Broadway, a man glided by on cross-country skis. The city streets were eerily silent.

Late in the afternoon, Jeremy phoned to suggest that I join him at a local restaurant for drinks. I could take Chris to a neighbor, he said. I found this proposal unusual but decided to go. Drinks were fine, a spontaneous change of pace. It was unexpected that Jeremy's partner join us, too, but fun. On our way home from the neighbor's, Christopher stuck his tongue out to catch snowflakes. His black bangs were studded with white.

"That was nice," I said to Jeremy, laying Chris on the kitchen counter to change his diapers. "What made you think of that little excursion?"

"Norman called me today with Finberg's decision," he said. "We lost."

Christopher giggled as I sprinkled baby powder on his bottom. "Mommy, some dinner?" I boiled water for a slice of sole, reheated some rice, threw in a handful of frozen peas. I felt as if I'd been punched.

The written decision arrived by messenger from Norman's office later that evening. Judge Finberg wrote that our "love, commitment, and care for Christopher, his affectionate acceptance by their extended families, and his development under their parenting has an unusually high quality," but that she "perceived constraint" by an earlier case, and "respondents were ordered to release the child to petitioner." The judge granted us a stay (Christopher would remain with us) until we applied to the Appellate Court if we wished to appeal her decision. Norman and Schwartz were to work out a weekly visitation arrangement for Angelina in our home.

Jeremy and I felt there was no choice. Norman appeared in front of an Appellate Court judge to request an appeal. We were granted another stay from this judge until our court date, probably several months away.

The first time Angelina saw Christopher he was twenty-two months old. It was a Sunday morning in April. The lawyers had decided that visitation should be one hour on Sundays. I requested an 11:00 A.M. appointment so that Christopher and I could go to Mass first.

Angelina followed me down the long hallway into the living room. She carried a Macy's shopping bag. Christopher sat playing with a Fisher-Price pop-up toy on the couch. Angelina sat down close to him. She pulled up one leg of Chris's overalls and pulled down his sock, rubbing his little calf.

"Beautiful," she said. "Beautiful legs."

"Beautiful shoes." My mother had bought Christopher

his first pair of real shoes, red leather with stitching on the toes. I called them his executive shoes.

"Beautiful socks," she said.

"Beautiful pantalons. Beautiful shirt." She fingered his white turtleneck.

"Beautiful baby," she pronounced finally.

I had absolutely no idea of what to say or do or think. Emily Post couldn't help me now. There was no chapter on what to serve when the biological mother visits. I just wished she would leave.

I remembered Jeremy saying a year earlier, "Well, if she wants him, she's going to have to come right here and take him out of his crib." And here she was.

Christopher remained perfectly calm. He didn't show any particular interest in Angelina. I wanted him to perform a little, to let her know how smart he was.

Angelina handed Christopher the Macy's box. He wouldn't take it, so finally I took it and pulled the ribbon off. A light blue dog. Tacky, I thought. Light blue is a terrible color for a dog. Angelina wound the dog up and we three sat stiffly, listening to "How Much Is That Doggie in the Window?" Jeremy stayed in the kitchen.

The pop-up toy had levers numbered 1, 2, 3, 4, 5. Donald Duck, Goofy, Pluto, Mickey Mouse, or Dumbo popped up depending on the number pushed. I pushed 3 for Goofy.

"Now you do it," I said to Christopher.

He sat.

"Okay," I said, "I'll do Donald Duck now."

"Good," said Angelina.

Christopher sat watching for ten minutes while Angelina and I congratulated each other on our pop-up skills.

Finally, I went into the bedroom and opened the window wide. Sticking my head far out, I took in several big gulps of cold air. In the kitchen, Jeremy banged the breakfast dishes around.

"An hour is up," he yelled out.

Back in the living room, Angelina watched Christopher trying to wind up the light blue dog.

"It's time to go," I said.

"OK," said Angelina, standing up immediately.

"Bye," she said to Christopher.

He didn't look up.

"Let's go somewhere," I said to Jeremy the second the elevator door closed. We drove up to Riverside Park. The sun was warm, springlike. Christopher straddled his Explorer, a six-wheeled bus about a foot high. His little legs pushed off from the pavement as fast as they could go. Zigzagging across the walk, his steering not quite coordinated with the car's speed, pumping the squeaking horn, Christopher was sheer happiness. "Why are you crying?" asked Jeremy, genuinely surprised.

"I love him too much," I said.

The next Sunday, Angelina was already walking down our block as we came home from church. "Hello, Lorenzo," she said to Christopher. Then, hopefully to me, "Maybe we go park?"

"No," I replied curtly.

I planted pansies in the living room window boxes, keeping myself occupied while spying on Angelina and Chris. When I thought of her calling him "Lorenzo," I found myself jabbing instead of spooning the dirt. I'd sneak a glance at them every few seconds. Christopher was absorbed with piling wooden blocks. Angelina seemed content to watch him, picking up the fallen blocks patiently and handing them back to him. "Beautiful flowers," she said to me. "How you call them?"

"Pansies," I said, "they're pansies."

"Pansies," she repeated slowly. "In my country, no pansies."

Angelina trailed behind me as I led Christopher into the kitchen to change his diapers. "When he baby," she said, "he have diarrhea?"

"No," I replied, thinking, what a weird question.

"Toast," said Christopher.

"Would you like some toast?" I asked Angelina. "Yes, please. Chris like bread?" She laughed. "Me, too. I like bread too much." She accepted a cup of coffee.

I was confused. Should I be offering her food? She wasn't a guest. We all wandered back to the living room. The bedroom door was closed as we passed; Jeremy was probably in there reading the Sunday paper. I yearned for a monitor; someone to enforce the rules. "An hour is up," I said.

"One hour," Angelina murmured, "so little." Her big black eyes looked at me pleadingly.

"That's the deal," I said, "one hour."

The next Sunday was Mother's Day. Angelina was supposed to call us on Saturday if she planned to visit on Sunday. She didn't phone, so Jeremy, Chris, and I set off in good conscience to a brunch to be prepared by the fathers of children in Christopher's play group.

A white bakery box filled with sugar cookies sat on the ledge over the mailboxes in our lobby when we came home in the afternoon. Written on the box in pencil: "For Maggie, Jeremy, and Baby. Angelina."

"Baby!" I snorted. "Should we throw these in the garbage?"

"I'll take them to my office tomorrow," said Jeremy. "They'll eat anything there. They're not bad," he added, extending the box to me.

Norman called the next morning. "Perez got married a few days ago in San Francisco."

"What! How do you know?"

"One of Finberg's law clerks told me."

"How would the law clerk know?"

"I don't know. But I have an idea. Do you speak Spanish?"

"No."

"Well, maybe somebody could tell you what to say in Spanish. Call Perez's apartment in San Francisco. Ask to speak to the wife. Tell her you're offering a free magazine subscription to new brides. Tape the conversation. We'll go back to court with it. They perjured themselves."

"Norman, I can't do that."

"Why not?"

"Because I can't."

"Maggie, we have to get this on tape."

"Well, why don't you call? What if she starts asking questions?"

"Okay, okay, I'll find a way. Meantime, you call Neil and see if he can check out the marriage license."

Neil had trouble getting clearance to open the sealed marriage license, but when he told the court officer the circumstances, he was permitted to photocopy the license and forward it to Family Court.

Norman's secretary made the phone call to Mrs. Perez, who not only giddily acknowledged her recent wedding but also volunteered the information that Perez had fathered their two children.

We returned to Family Court a few weeks later for a rehearing of these new facts. During the interim, Angelina had not phoned or visited on Sundays. In court, the interpreter translated a letter received from Perez's sister:

"Angelina, the motive for this letter is to tell you about the problem of my brother, Rafael. Immigration got to him and they kept him several days detained, but my aunt Louisa gave him bail and he came out on the bail, but the lawyer counseled him to marry as soon as possible. So, in order to see if he can fix things up and for that reason, he had to get married. And since you did not let us know anything, he found himself corralled and he had to have recourse to that which was nearer to him."

Angelina seemed unperturbed by the loss of her potential husband. On the stand again, she announced a new plan. She would live with Perez's sister in San Francisco, but had little or no idea of the sister's living and marital arrangements and the reasons her own children lived apart from her.

Judge Finberg's findings and conclusions on the rehearing stated, "The conclusion is inescapable. To grant custody to petitioner means that the child will go from a stable, secure, devoted two-parent home, in which loving attention to his development has been a priority from birth, to unsettled, precarious, shifting, unpredictable care. Petitioner does not even have an assured place of residence for him. . . . There are such grave reasons to conclude that the child would be harmed by transfer of custody to the mother that it is difficult if not impossible to reconcile the interests of the mother and the child on the basis of the rule that 'both interests . . . ordinarily converge.' "

Judge Finberg exonerated Jeremy and me from guilt by stating "petitioner-mother's right is diminished by the fact that she freely, voluntarily, and deliberately placed the child in respondents' custody for the purpose of their adopting him; his predicament is due to her conduct."

The judge continued, "On the other hand, however, the Court of Appeals recently stated that 'parental custody of a child may not be displaced absent grievous cause or necessity' and indicated that a parent is only 'disqualified by gross misconduct.' Solely on the constraint of that ruling, the petition for custody is again granted and respondents are ordered to release the child to petitioner."

We again sought and were granted a stay by the Appellate Division pending appeal.

It is not unusual to retain a new attorney for an appeal. We were recommended to a lawyer in a large, established Wall Street firm.

"Everyone has a price," Carl Belzer said flatly. "Have you offered her money?"

"I don't think she wants money," I said.

"Has it been discussed?" asked Carl.

"No," said Jeremy.

"Someone should broach the issue," he said. "Twenty thousand now and ten thousand a year for the next ten years. Something like that."

Another attorney said no after speaking with me for only ten minutes. We later discovered he had recently defended biological parents against foster parents in the Supreme Court. Leonard Boudin, an attorney with his own daughter's future in serious jeopardy (Kathy Boudin had been jailed after surfacing as one of the Weatherpeople involved in a Brinks robbery), turned us down regretfully.

We decided on Miriam Friedman, a professor at Columbia University Law School. Miriam taught courses in family law and had previous experience working in Family Court. She was articulate, sympathetic, straightforward, and reasonable. She was also extremely overworked and proposed hiring another attorney to help her research for the brief. We met Jeffrey Laef and were satisfied with the prospective collaboration.

Miriam and Jeffrey's job would be to write a brief supporting our position, drawing on testimony from the Family Court trial as well as citing earlier legal cases.

When the brief was submitted to the Appellate Division, we would be given a court date for oral arguments.

In order for the attorneys to review the trial proceedings, it was necessary to order typewritten transcripts from the stenographer's tapes. The stenographers were different for almost every court appearance, and some of them were now working in another borough or were on vacation. Christopher and I rode my bike down to Family Court several times that summer in an effort to expedite transcript production. Chris was belted into the molded seat behind me, his head encased in a plastic helmet. It was tempting to look for Judge Finberg's chambers and confront her, but we didn't.

Angelina went to the Midwest for several weeks with her employers, so we enjoyed a tranquil August renting on Long Island again. After a few months of a rather limited vocabulary, including *DaDo* and *Mama*, words now began spilling out of Christopher like a waterfall. When he said "yellow," his tongue came straight out of his mouth and licked his upper lip, like he was trying to catch a fly. We couldn't resist making him say "yellow" to everyone who would listen, or, more accurately, watch.

His rendering of dump truck was "bump da"; our neighbor's son Anthony, "Anna." Anthony was six and had been delighted to spend a weekend with us on Long Island just after Christopher's second birthday. Anthony's mother, Kathy, often babysat for Chris. Kathy volunteered Anthony to serve as a role model for Chris's toilet training. Over the weekend, Anthony would periodically urinate into a large Tupperware container. Kathy assured me that this was The Method for boys. Christopher watched Anthony gravely, then said, "No pee in Anna's cup." He proceeded to urinate in his shorts whenever he chose but never in the cup. After a few days of this approach, I decided he wasn't ready yet and laid in a supply of Pampers.

Fluke, sand shark, blowfish, flounder, swordfish, halibut, weakfish, corn on the cob, and tomatoes were the mainstays of our August diet. Every night we'd barbecue our fish on the hibachi and eat dinner on the porch watching the sunset blaze through the trees until the mosquitoes got too fierce for us to stay outdoors. Family and friends came and went. Images: Christopher in his red Dr. Dentons, framed by my nieces in their long, flowered nightgowns, picking raspberries early one dewy morning for Jeremy's famed fruit pancakes. The Greenport Band Concert (bring your own chair), complete with tubas and triangles, and Christopher dancing in little circles, his sun-browned cheeks flushed, his black eyes snapping in the town street lights. Jeremy and Chris, arms entwined, napping together in the creaky old double bed that smelled of mothballs.

One of Chris's second birthday presents was an inflatable, bright green plastic turtle lying on its back. I supported my head on the turtle's head and my arms and legs on the turtle's stubs. Securing Christopher on my lap with one arm and using the other arm as a paddle, I'd steer the turtle over the shore waves. Even when we tipped over and his mouth filled with saltwater, Christopher came up laughing.

Sunning on the beach one Sunday with various houseguests, I pulled a New York *Post* from a stack of newspapers. One large photograph filled the front page: a closeup of a teary-eyed couple with their arms around a tot of perhaps two. The caption read: "Adoptive Parents Surrender Child to Real Mom." I clawed through the paper for details, but there was no interior reference to the photo. That could be us someday.

I looked at Christopher, stalking seagulls while sucking

on an orange juice popsicle, nude, his white bottom a sharp contrast to his tanned chest and sturdy brown thighs, his black hair this summer a tangle of curls. A deep pain spread through my chest as the guests argued about whether or not the water was warm enough for swimming.

One hot afternoon just before Labor Day, when Christopher and my mother were napping, Jeremy phoned from the city. Norman had just called him with a new decision from Judge Finberg. She had reversed her decision. We had won custody of Christopher! I wandered back and forth in tight little circles through the cottage. How could this be true? Though I'd given up smoking some ten years earlier, I longed for a cigarette. Finally my mother woke up. Telling her made it seem more real. We laughed and cried, hugging each other tightly.

Jeremy called back. No, we hadn't won. Norman had sent the new memorandum on to Jeffrey and a more careful reading indicated that Judge Finberg had stayed with her original verdict. She was proposing to the Appellate Division that *they* use their higher powers to decide in our favor. She wrote that our continuing custody—even absent the possibility of adoption—"appears to be the least detrimental alternative from the standpoint of the child's welfare." Also, she noted that removal of Christopher from our home "presents an unprecedented question of a child's constitutional right to the State's concern for his welfare." She concluded: "In the instant case the danger to the child's welfare from a transfer of custody to his mother is so unmistakable that their interests cannot be reconciled on the basis of a presumed convergence."

She couldn't quite do it herself, though. She perceived the "restraint expected of a lower court." In essence, Judge Finberg invited the Appellate Court to assume the

responsibility of a decision to leave Christopher with us.
"She's a coward," said Jeremy. "I hope she has trouble
sleeping the rest of her life."

In the fall Angelina came over most Mondays. The
appellate judge who granted the stay had increased visiting time to six hours a week, from 10:00 A.M. to 4:00
P.M., on either Sunday or Monday, Angelina's days off.
Jeremy suggested that she come on Mondays so we could
have weekends to ourselves.

Christopher and I would have an early morning outing
to air ourselves and dissipate my anxiety. Angelina usually arrived about 11:00. She and Chris would play in his
room, a large, bright, open section in the north end of
our loft. I don't know what Angelina said to Chris when
they were alone. I couldn't hear much talking. If Christopher laughed, I felt spasms of jealousy. I invented
reasons to appear in his room—to water the plants, put
away laundry. Mondays became the day to scrub the
quarry tile floor, vacuum the carpets—take on any physical labor to absorb frustration.

Christopher liked Angelina. Why shouldn't he? Other
adults who came to our house played with him for a while
but eventually turned their attention to Jeremy or me in
various parts of the house. Angelina was different. Her
presence was restricted to Christopher's room, her focus
reserved for him. She never asked for anything, not even
to use the bathroom.

She never suggested any variations in the routine. She
began to bring food now and then, not every week, but
often. Small cans of fruit punch, strawberries (a favorite
of Christopher's), broccoli, another. When she brought a
large box of sugared breakfast cereal and several other
food items, I fumed around the kitchen for a while (my
tolerance for the empty calories of sugar cereals is low),

then set the grocery bag by the elevator door. "We have our own food," I said. "Please take this home." Angelina nodded yes.

Theo, my therapist neighbor, explained to me that giving food is nurturing. What more basic approach could Angelina use than to fill Christopher up? The food bothered me. Perhaps Angelina understood; she stopped bringing it.

She hovered while I rocked Christopher for his afternoon nap. Self-conscious about singing lullabies with an audience, I intoned "Winnie the Pooh" or "Allouetta" without energy. Then I was angry that Angelina could affect me in this way—in any way.

Jeremy started coming home for lunch on Mondays. He and Christopher and I would eat sitting around the butcherblock dining table just off Chris's room. Attempts to make the meal festive were compounded by my heightened consciousness of Angelina's pointed exclusion. Christopher would call out, "Analina, I'm having my lunch." She'd murmur, "Good, Chris."

One hot September Monday, Jeremy and I stood chatting in the kitchen after lunch. I glanced into the mirror that reflects into Christopher's room; his body whizzed by in a blue sunsuit. He'd been wearing a red sunsuit. "She changed him," I said to Jeremy. "She changed his clothes."

Jeremy stalked into Chris's room and said to Angelina in a loud strained voice, "Don't touch his clothes. He's our child." Angelina handed Jeremy the wet red sunsuit and pointed to an empty plastic container that had been filled with water for painting.

I was embarrassed at Jeremy's tone with Angelina yet struck by the pain in his words. His reaction was so dramatic and telling. Jeremy meant to protect Christopher, and Angelina threatened Jeremy. "He's our child" was a primal, territorial statement. Jeremy had no positive way to express his suffering. Lashing out at Angelina over a sunsuit was one way of saying, "You're hurting me."

And I had pushed him into confronting her. I felt guilty that I hadn't handled the situation myself. Retreating behind Jeremy, who was expected, conditioned, as a man, to be strong, that is, not to show pain, was unfair.

I was relieved, though, that Angelina hadn't changed Chris's sunsuit arbitrarily and pleased that he was out of his wet clothes. Exhausted and confused after another Monday.

Jeremy's overall response to Angelina was animosity. There was no middle ground. He felt that she had done something so monumentally unforgivable that it would compromise him even to acknowledge her existence. Recognizing her would be tantamount to condoning her behavior. His imperative not to touch Christopher's clothes was the first time he had spoken to Angelina.

I could sense Angelina's fear of Jeremy. In a way, I wasn't sure if he should come home for lunch on Mondays. The strain and tension of the meal were draining. It seemed unfair to leave Angelina out—foolish, maybe. We had been wronged and we were wounded. But depriving her of sharing lunch was a hollow revenge.

CHAPTER
Twelve

I availed myself of opportunities to vent my anxieties. I had Patrick, the priest, and his church. I had Theo, my therapist neighbor. My three sisters. Friends. Jeremy kept his feelings to himself. In the hopes that he might release some of his anxiety in the spiritual and psychological presences of Patrick and Theo, I set up a dinner for the four of us. We shared a lovely evening, but the conversation never got around to Angelina. Patrick and Jeremy talked mostly about urban renewal, while Theo spoke of her upcoming trip to India. I should have known better than to attempt staging a catharsis.

Patrick said he wanted to talk with Angelina. The next Monday when she visited, she agreed with a sort of "why not?" shrug, and I walked her around the block to the church. Patrick called me a few hours later to report that he had spoken with Angelina at length. From her Spanish he thought she was quite well-educated. She spoke of a future with friends in Mill Valley and didn't mention the biological father. She assured Patrick that even if she went hungry, Christopher would always have enough to eat. When Patrick asked how she felt about disrupting our lives, Angelina didn't have an answer. She looked down at her lap and looked sad. She wanted to know what we thought of her. She told Patrick she wasn't a bad person. I wished I could have eavesdropped on their conversation. I knew so little about Angelina, every tidbit of information was savored.

I had hoped that more would come of their meeting, but I was grateful for Patrick's concern. Jeremy, on the other hand, was annoyed because he thought Patrick should have been more influential with Angelina.

Theo often came down to chat on Mondays. She peered into the mirror that reflects into Chris's room in an attempt to observe Angelina. Angelina seemed to manage to position herself just out of view. "You need a bigger mirror," said Theo. "You could make him hate her," she said. "You could condition him. Get a picture of Angelina and show it to him over and over. Say 'Angelina is bad. Angelina is poo poo.' It could work."

"Theo," I sighed. "I can't do that. What if he does have to go off with her some day? I can't make him hate her."

"I would," she said.

"Well, I can't. Let's think of something more constructive."

"Okay," she said, "since you asked. I see a behavior pattern in you. You tend to wait until things happen to you. You have to take charge yourself. I don't think you've completely checked out your own potential to bear a child. Why don't you see a fertility specialist? Make sure you've done everything possible. Then you won't have any regrets ten years down the road."

The endocrinological infertility specialist was surprised that my previous treatment hadn't included a postcoital test. Jeremy and I were to have intercourse the following Sunday morning at seven and I was to appear at the hospital for examination by eight. Dr. Seiden invited me to peer through the microscope at Jeremy's sperm squiggling around my cervical mucus. He proclaimed that all looked well. Considering my gynecological history, he recommended I try *in vitro* fertilization, but he was still in the process of hiring a critical team member for his program in New York. A colleague in Houston was conducting a successful *in vitro* program; Dr. Seiden could get me into the program right away. I put that consideration on hold; Texas seemed so far away for the risky venture of a test-tube baby.

Jeremy and I mused about adopting another baby. I called Norman and tentatively broached the issue. "Sure," he said, "I have a Southern girl expecting in two weeks, but she doesn't want any Catholics or Jews for parents. Are you sure Jeremy's not Episcopalian?"

Norman told me to call him when we were certain that we were ready for another baby. I guess he detected some hesitation in us, some trepidation of another backfire. And Christopher was only two and a half; we were enjoying his only-child status. I wasn't sure we were ready for number two.

We visited Jeremy's parents in St. Louis. Grandpa Ryan is a gentle man with an extraordinary amount of patience. He donned a striped engineer's hat and escorted Christopher to the basement to introduce him to Jeremy's old electric train. They spent hours together during the following week. Christopher proved to be a careful conductor, speeding up on the straightaway but always slowing into a curve. He handled reverse as well as forward. When a car derailed, Christopher put it meticulously back on the tracks. By the second day, he had figured out the switch system for four tracks. Jeremy and Christopher toured a train museum and Chris returned with his own striped cap and a wood whistle for Grandpa. Chris's careful, patient approach to life aligned perfectly with his grandfather's character.

Grandma Ryan has myeloma, cancer of the blood. Periods of intense pain alternate without warning with shorter periods of relief. Sometimes she takes as many as nineteen pills a day. Her immune system has deteriorated so that she is susceptible to various other illnesses. Most of the time she sits in a recliner chair in the living room with a pillow behind her back and another pillow under her.

Our visit was a tonic for Grandma. She patiently repeated colors over and over with Christopher until he could differentiate between dark blue and light blue. He sat on her bed while she rested, and they watched "Sesame Street" together.

Jeremy's parents were baffled by our situation. They always wanted to know where Angelina got her money, how she had paid for her lawyer. We didn't know the answers either.

We brought Jeremy's Lionel train back to New York with us, but it wasn't the same without Grandpa.

I investigated several nursery schools for the fall. After Christopher and I spent a morning there, I chose the Montessori school on our block. The director patiently led Chris through the routine, giving him a chance to show her what he could do. He poured water from one pitcher into another without spilling, figured out a puzzle, arranged blocks by size, fed the gerbil, climbed to the top of the playhouse, and slid down the slide, all with quiet competence. He looked shyly at the other children. I looked forward to his starting school in six months.

In March, Jim's brother offered us two weeks at his time-share condominium in Maui. We were delighted at this sunlit winter escape and stopped off first for a few days in Honolulu to pick up my sister and her family, who joined us in Maui. The kids loved the ocean, the beach, sleeping together. My sister and I hadn't spent so much time together since we had been children.

We sat on the sand watching Jeremy and Christopher jump about in the ocean waves. "Jeremy is a good father," said Ann. "He sure loves Chris."

"Yes," I said, "there's no doubt about that."

Watching Jeremy indulge my nephew gave me a glimpse of a future Christopher and his dad. Charles, aged nine, wanted to try out every sport available at the compound, but he needed a partner. Jeremy was ever-available to play tennis, shuffleboard, croquet, while Ann and I sat chatting or dangling our feet in the pool.

"I talked to Jeremy down at the barbecue pit last night," said Ann. "He has so much anger in him, I really feel sorry for him. It must be hard to endure."

I hadn't thought of his anger in quite that way. I'd been thinking of how hard it was for *me* to endure.

"Somewhere in the Bible it says that God doesn't give us more than we can endure," said Ann. "I pray all the time for the three of you. It just has to work out."

Our new lawyers for the Appellate Court appearance, Miriam and Jeffrey, had submitted our brief in January in order that our case might be heard in the spring term. The written argument was based on two points: that Christopher would be at substantial risk of severe and lasting psychological damage if removed from our custody, and that Family Court had erred in excluding extrinsic evidence of Angelina's adoption intention.

Judge Finberg had just retired. She was seventy. Ironically, she was consulting at Columbia University Law School, where Miriam taught. Finberg told Miriam that the information that Perez had married someone else had been given to her law clerk by the interpreter. Angelina must have come to trust the interpreter and confided in her. The interpreter evidently felt it was her duty to report this new information to the judge. Miriam said that Judge Finberg hoped we'd win in the Appellate Division.

The Appellate Division of the Supreme Court is far grander than Family Court. The large, ornate room has an old world elegance about it. Gold-framed oil portraits of decades of black-robed judges line the walls. Mahogany railings separate the attorneys and the judges from the spectators.

Fifteen male judges comprise the Appellate Division; five of these form the panel hearing cases on any given day. Miriam had said the identity of our five would depend on the luck of the draw. Their names would be announced the morning of our court appearance.

The judges had reviewed the Family Court testimony as well as the brief. No new testimony would be given in Appellate Court; our roles this time were those of observers. After Miriam and Schwartz presented their twenty-five-minute oral arguments, the judges could interrogate them as they wished.

The Appellate Court is open to the public. I sat between Jeremy and my sister Katherine, who had flown in from Chicago to be with us in court. Our friends Elaine and Theo came along as well as Jeremy's partners, Peter and John. I was grateful for Katherine's presence, especially since she'd be staying for three days, but I didn't know whether it was better or worse to have all the others there as well. It was important to them to be with us, however.

Angelina came in late with Jorge Cabas, the process server. She was dressed somberly in a navy blue suit. I pointed her out to Katherine, who said after scrutinizing her, "She looks mean." Her observation was cruel, but I appreciated her bias, needing her solidarity.

An oral argument provides a shining dramatic moment for an attorney. Miriam's voice was a bit shaky as she began, but her confidence built quickly and she carried through to a persuasive, convincing crescendo. Jeffrey sat a few yards behind Miriam, the foot-high pile of testimony on the chair next to him.

Judge Caronia asked Miriam most of the questions, focusing on Angelina's illegal alien status. Caronia wondered about the possibility that Angelina wanted custody of Christopher to obtain American citizenship for herself.

Judge Weyl zeroed in on Angelina's poverty, holding it up as if to admire it. He asserted that there are thousands of single working mothers in New York City who are raising children. "I bet he had a poor childhood," whispered Katherine. Weyl said poverty is not a disqualification for successful parenting.

Weyl also discredited the testimony of Dr. Krinski, the child psychiatrist who had so impressed Judge Finberg in Family Court, by claiming that experts compensated by only one side express opinions that are too subjective.

Judge Powell presented his view that the best interests of Christopher were indeed the issue and that Christopher's age at present, three years, and the fact that he had been with Jeremy and me his whole life, were crucial. He also worried that Angelina might voluntarily return to El Salvador, termed unsafe for Americans by the United States State Department just the previous week.

In his oral argument, Schwartz seized the cue on poverty and stressed Angelina's economic straits, claiming that Jeremy and I had used our "financial superiority" to stonewall her. Jorge Cabas, sitting with Angelina in the row in front of us, turned around and glared at Jeremy and me. I returned his stare but felt a flush rise up my cheeks.

Schwartz claimed our case could be decided on the basis of *Sanjavini*, a case in which the child's age was determined to be unimportant because much of his life had already been spent in litigation. Schwartz pounded on the podium to emphasize his points, his voice thick with sarcasm. He said that Jeremy and I tried to take the law into our own hands and that our attitude should give pause as to the values we might be likely to inculcate into Christopher.

The fourth judge claimed that if we were allowed to continue to have custody, without adoption, the Court would be accomplishing by legal fiat what King Solomon only threatened to accomplish by sword.

The presiding judge didn't ask any questions.

It was over. As we milled about the vestibule, Miriam introduced us to her mother, who had been in the gallery. I was genuinely touched that she had come.

Jeremy's firm had designed a nearby restaurant, so he took us all out for lunch after court. The general mood was optimistic; it was difficult to be somber lunching with nine people. Miriam thought a verdict would come in four to eight weeks.

After lunch Katherine and I picked Christopher up from the babysitter's, changed into jeans, and went to the park for ice cream cones. While Chris played in the sandbox, Katherine and I rehashed the morning's events. We were encouraged by the tone of the judge's questions. They seemed to take Judge Finberg's disquiet seriously.

Christopher's third birthday was to be his first real party, with guests his own age, from his play group and his babysitter's clientele. The menu was a matter of grave concern to me. Spaghetti? Too messy and too hot for July. Hamburgers? Too much last-minute work. My friend Kay proposed the perfect solution. First we trimmed the crust from a loaf of white bread. Then we pressed down metal cookie cutters to transform the sliced rectangles into horses, cows, and rabbits. Egg salad, tuna fish, and peanut butter and jelly provided the interiors of our animal sandwiches. Carrot sticks and apple juice completed the entree.

The afternoon before the party, while Christopher and I were debating over pink or green frosting for the cupcakes, Jeremy phoned with the Appellate Court decision.

Angelina had won, three to two.

I had resolved not to cry about this in front of Christopher. I went in the bathroom and turned the cold water on. I sat on the toilet.

Chris came to the bathroom door. "What's wrong, Mom? A booboo?"

"Chris, Chris, Chris." I swooped him up. "I do love you."

"Why are you crying, Mom?"

"Chris, I love you so much sometimes it makes me cry. Isn't that silly?"

"Yes, you're silly, Mom."

Christopher wore his sailor suit for the party. Alexandra, David, Andrew, Margo, Anthony, and Christopher crowded around the papier-mâché panda bear piñata suspended with rope from a sprinkler pipe and stuffed with mini-boxes of raisins, plastic watches, Hot Wheels cars, Chinese purses, and Hershey's chocolate kisses. None of the blindfolded children were strong enough to make a dent in the bear with a plastic baseball bat. Finally Jeremy whacked the bear with a broom, and one leg dangled down. As the children scrambled on the floor for treats, the doorbell buzzed.

"Let me up, Maggie, let me up." Theo's voice was hysterical, almost incomprehensible. "I saw it on the subway. In the newspaper. Let me up."

Damn. Now I would have to comfort Theo. I had put off telling her the verdict because I knew her reaction would exhaust me.

"Omigod, Maggie. You can't imagine. The woman next to me on the subway. I grabbed the paper from her hand. Did you see this?" Theo waved the *Daily News* in my face. David's mother stared at us.

Christopher ran into the kitchen. "Why is Theo crying, Mom?" He looked alarmed.

"Theo," I said softly, pulling her into our bedroom, away from the party. "Please calm down a little. You're frightening Christopher." I put my arms around her until the wailing subsided.

I scanned the article, headlined: ORDER TOT RETURNED TO ILLEGAL ALIEN MOM. The majority judge wrote, "If the natural mother is compelled to return to El Salvador without her son, it would mean that she will be permanently separated from him. He would be exiled from his natural family and his cultural heritage. Certainly, in El Salvador, there are children who flourish. It is even argued by some that New York is a more dangerous place to grow up."

The article said Angelina could not be reached for comment, but her lawyer said the decision "upholds the sanctity of the mother–child relationship."

A television reporter called the next day. Anticipating the call, I was able to talk somewhat calmly about our case and said we might consider an interview if I could be convinced of a good reason for it, other than just serving as a dramatic guaranteed tear-jerker. It would not be possible to include Christopher in the interview, I told the reporter. There was no reason to subject him to that ordeal.

"Frankly," he said, "I know what my editor would say. You gotta have the kid. There's no story without the kid."

"Sure," I said. "I understand." Our transaction was concluded.

In the twenty-six-page opinion, the majority judge had written six pages; the two dissenting judges, a total of twenty pages. Judge Caronia wrote: "Rodriguez's circumstances are not even comparable to that of other poor unwed mothers, since the latter generally have certain community and personal resources at their disposal. It was her recognition of just that fact—that she lacked the emotional sustenance or family environment necessary for the proper maintenance of a child—that induced her to relinquish her son in the first place."

Jeffrey told Jeremy a court clerk had said that at one point during the Appellate Court deliberations the presiding judge of the five-man jury had been on our side, but ultimately he was converted to Angelina's position. So at one point we had won; at another moment we had lost.

The majority assumed that the best interests of Christopher were irrelevant so long as Angelina, the "innocent parent," was not clearly unfit. It assumed that biology is the most important criterion for motherhood. It dismissed the fact that Angelina had surrendered Christopher, and nowhere did it explain how the best interests of Christopher would be served by the return. As one minority judge wrote, "To send him to Rodriguez and to an unstable future might serve respondent's needs. The child, however, will certainly be harmed."

We were allowed another appeal, to New York's highest

court, the Court of Appeals in Albany. Essentially, we'd repeat the process we'd just been through, submitting a revised brief and preparing a fresh oral argument. Again a stay was granted. We'd probably go to Albany in six months.

At Miriam Friedman's suggestion, I contacted a child psychiatrist with whom she worked at Columbia University. I met with Dr. Lillian Eidelstein a few times, taking Jeremy with me once. Dr. Eidelstein felt that we were doing as much as we could do until the court reached a decision. In the meantime, she suggested that I hire a Spanish babysitter and try to have Christopher learn some Spanish. She knew a bilingual social worker and thought that Angelina and I might both meet with this woman around the time that we would be going to the Court of Appeals.

Angelina had been out of town when the verdict came. She resumed her Monday visits in the fall. We never discussed the decision. Her English remained rudimentary, and our typical exchange might be about the delicious strawberries or tomatoes she'd consumed while in Michigan with her employers.

Thirteen

We hadn't planned ahead sufficiently and so were unable to rent a cottage that summer. Christopher and I enjoyed various city outings—basically covering the nearby parks with occasional forays to the Bronx Zoo, Fire Island beaches, and the Museum of Natural History. By the end of August we were all hot and cranky and ready for a change.

Friends invited us to join them at a rented summer house at Lake Tahoe. I wasn't sure Angelina understood when I told her about our plans. As usual, when I told her we were going away, she was confused about when we were to be home again. I got my big wall calendar down and focused on clarifying the dates. The fact that we'd be traveling on an airplane to a faraway place always seemed secondary to her concern for the return date, when she would come over again. I was never sure she knew where we were going.

Lake Tahoe was sunny yet cool, with tall pine trees punctuating the cloudless blue horizon. It was good to see our friends again. Jeremy particularly enjoyed this group, four men with whom he'd gone to high school in Chicago. The women had become friends, too. Everyone made a big fuss over Christopher, and it was fun for him to play with our friends' children.

Jeremy, Christopher, and I went on alone to spend four days in Yosemite National Park, staying two nights in a little cabin in the woods and two nights in a beautiful old Indian hotel. We hiked, swam, petted deer, picnicked, rose at dawn to see a spectacular sunrise from a mountaintop. Christopher was easy to travel with; an only child is almost a luxury.

But I had always wanted more than one child. Growing up with three sisters and two brothers had been intense, textured. My childhood memories were warm, rich ones. Now, as adults, my three sisters were my best friends. Any time my family gathered together was special, an event to be anticipated.

I wanted Christopher to be a big brother. He had already turned three. We didn't want much more of an age difference between Chris and a brother or sister. And we didn't want to be much older ourselves when we added another child to our family.

A new baby in the house might deflect some of the attention and anxiety that we felt about Christopher. I knew, too, though I didn't really want to think about it too much, that if the day ever came when Christopher had to leave us, we would be devastated. If we had a new baby, someone who needed us, we wouldn't be allowed to lapse into emotional lethargy.

My infertility specialist counseled me to keep trying to get pregnant, to pursue *in vitro*, and to investigate another adoption. "So maybe you'll end up with three kids," he said. "You'd have one *in vitro*, you'd adopt another one, and you'd still have Christopher."

After six months under the infertility specialist's care,

which included three postcoital examinations, hormones to induce ovulation, and pills to cure infections, I wasn't pregnant. Jeremy and I talked it through and decided to go ahead with investigative surgery for *in vitro* fertilization. Dr. Seiden called his colleague at the *in vitro* clinic in Houston and introduced me. The timing was right in my menstrual cycle, and I could tack the trip to Texas onto the end of our Western vacation.

From Reno, Jeremy and Christopher flew to St. Louis to visit Grandma and Grandpa Ryan. On the flight to Houston, I listened to the "Goldberg Variations" on my Walkman while reading *The Clan of the Cave Bear*. From the airport I went straight to Dr. Wright's office, where she examined me and discussed the next morning's procedure. Then I enjoyed a Chinese dinner at a restaurant near my hotel and stayed up late to finish my book. The solitude was such a delightful change that I didn't even feel nervous about the upcoming surgery.

The screening laparoscopy performed the following morning was to see whether my ovaries were accessible for egg retrieval. The fallopian tube that had been reimplanted during my surgery four years earlier was not to be found, and one ovary was blocked. But the other ovary was accessible, so I could be accepted into the program.

If I elected to enter the program, I would have to return to Houston within three months, on day five of my menstrual cycle. Ultrasound monitoring of follicular growth would begin on cycle day ten, followed by laparoscopy for follicular aspiration (taking the egg from the ovary) between cycle days fourteen and seventeen. I would have to remain in Houston for three to four days following the laparoscopy. Jeremy would have to be available at least on the day of laparoscopy and the following day. His sperm, obtained by masturbation, would be mixed with the egg to allow fertilization to occur. Then the egg would be transferred into a different medium for growth, and after several cell divisions, if the embryo was developing normally, it would be transferred into my uterus by means of a small tube inserted through my cervix.

The fee for each treatment would be $3,500 and the chance of successful implantation on the first try was 15 percent. Most insurance companies considered *in vitro* fertilization to be experimental or in the nature of research and would not provide any reimbursement for expenses incurred in the actual attempt.

Flying back to New York that afternoon, I pondered. My chances of success with *in vitro* seemed extremely slim. Traveling back and forth to Houston, particularly with Christopher about to start nursery school, seemed preposterous. Somehow, having had the investigative surgery was enough for me. I told Dr. Seiden we'd pursue another child through private adoption.

A month or so later Dr. Seiden phoned to ask whether Jeremy and I would be interested in adopting the baby of a newly referred teenaged patient from Connecticut. We accepted. After a few weeks I pressed him for details, and he told me that when the girl had finally got the courage to tell her mother about the baby, her mother told her for the first time that she, too, was adopted! Her mother had adopted her through Catholic Charities in Connecticut, and as that was the route she wanted her daughter to follow, we were out of the picture.

Meanwhile, Dr. Seiden had attended an infertility convention and secured the names of centers that introduced surrogate mothers to prospective parents. I called the appropriately named Hagar Institute in Kentucky for information. The initial interview, which would last several hours and include other couples, would cost $400.

The tone of the literature made me feel as if we might be attending an EST seminar. The entire process, including payment to the surrogate and a lawyer's fee, would cost a minimum of $25,000. Jeremy and I suspected that a surrogate mother, who was actually choosing to become pregnant, might be a stronger candidate for a change of mind than a pregnant biological mother, who chose adoption.

Theo urged me to ask one of my sisters to be a surrogate for me. "I can't think of a greater gift of love than making a baby for your sister," she said. My oldest sister, Katherine, had recently married a divorced father of three who, at age 46, had undergone a vasectomy reversal for Katherine. They were trying to have a child of their own. My sister Ann, a mother of two in Hawaii, had had her tubes tied years earlier. My sister Helen, in Miami, mother of two boys, ten and twelve, seemed the most likely prospect. But before I had time to ask her to consider carrying her brother-in-law's child, she confided that she was pregnant. She went on to tell me that she had undergone two miscarriages in the past three years and that when amniosentesis had shown that she was carrying a child with Down's Syndrome, she and her family had suffered through the tortuous decision to terminate the pregnancy. Finally she had conceived a healthy baby. Though we are close, she hadn't told me about all her pregnancies because of our situation with Christopher. None of my sisters could help us have a baby.

We decided to pursue a second private adoption, this time with Norman Bernstein as our lawyer. The usual route that Norman recommended was for prospective adoptive parents to place an ad in the Miscellaneous section of a small newspaper, something like,

ADOPTION

Happily married, financially secure, white young couple will
give your baby a loving, warm home. All expenses paid.
Confidential. (Phone number.)

When the biological mother reading the ad called the
adoptive parents, they would direct her to Norman. Thus
instead of Norman introducing the parties, the situation
would be brought to him. Because of our problems with
Christopher, we had priority over the usual route. A
college student in Colorado, who had already gone
through one private adoption with Norman, was expecting her second child and had contacted Norman directly.
She would give birth at about the time the Appeals Court
decision would be coming down, a few months before
Christopher's fourth birthday. Norman assured us she
was rational, reliable, her education a priority. We gave
him $2,000 for her living and medical expenses.

Christopher started nursery school in the fall. He loved
everything about it—the director, the other children, his
lunch box. In the bathtub he'd hum snatches of songs
learned at school. He knew his alphabet, could count to
twenty. It was exciting to see him take off.

I never told anyone at the nursery school that Christopher is adopted. It's not that I was trying to hide it. It
just never came up. With his Prince Valiant haircut and
his jeans and rugby shirts, he looks like any kid in a
Cheerios commercial. He idolizes Mr. T, can beat me at
"Memory," and puts ketchup on green beans. He is our
son. Who could doubt it?

Casual questions dropped in random conversations with
other mothers, perhaps while watching our children in
the park. "Would you ever have another one?" or "Did
you have a Caesarean?" were easy enough to circumvent,

the first with evasive, noncommital murmurings, the second with "no," which was true enough. A New York type of privacy prevails, even among mothers of small children.

Everyone said how much he looked like me. It was the hair mostly—dark brown with a streak of auburn here and there in sunlight—and the dark eyes. He sounded like me, too, echoing my frequent "actually" and "also" and requesting "peace and quiet" as he closed the bathroom door.

Maybe I *was* trying to hide Christopher's adoption, come to think of it. I liked his looking and talking like me. It was easier that way.

We spent Thanksgiving in St. Louis with Jeremy's family, Christmas in Chicago with mine. Christopher in black velvet shorts and white knee socks, wide-eyed at his first performance of *The Nutcracker*. Chris treating his cousins to a matinee of *Return of the Jedi*. Chris cross-country skiing in my brother's backyard, the extension of a golf course.

We drove from Chicago back to our newly purchased farmhouse in the Catskill Mountains, three hours north of New York City. Visiting friends in the area the previous fall, we had decided to look at houses for sale. This was the first one we had seen. It was on three acres of land and had a trout stream out back, ten enormous Norway spruce trees in the yard, an upstairs and a downstairs, a wood-burning stove in the kitchen, and a fireplace in the living room. The house was over one hundred years old and had been owned by only one family. It needed lots of work, but it was ridiculously inexpensive and had enormous potential.

We spent January and February weekends cracking up the lineoleum floors to expose the yellow pine wood planks underneath. We frequented local auctions for antiques. The previous owner had left an old wooden sled in the barn for Christopher, and Jeremy pulled him down the snowy driveway. Chris and I lay on our backs and made angels in the snow.

The fireplace backed up and covered the whole house, including the manuscript I was copyediting, with fine gray soot. I spent hours stripping layers of white paint from a pine Hoosier cabinet in the kitchen. Jeremy knocked down a kitchen wall and redesigned the room, exposing the wood beams in the ceiling. We poured our energy into restoration.

Suddenly it was February 20, our Court of Appeals date in Albany. My sister Katherine and her husband, Philip, came in from Chicago to be with us at court. We spent the weekend in the country, two-thirds of the distance between New York City and Albany.

Christopher woke up crying in the middle of Sunday night, as if he knew something was going on. Even though the space heater was on in his room, it was cold. The lineoleum floor, not yet stripped in the bedrooms, felt like ice on my bare feet. I brought Chris into bed with Jeremy and me, snuggling him between us. When his breathing was even and his sleep restored, a sudden anxiety washed over me. I couldn't get back to sleep. The swish of an occasional passing car, the sweep of the headlights making shadows on the wall, the whir of the oil burner in the basement, the scurry of mice in the attic, measured the night until light and a thick snowfall were visible through the uncurtained windows. It was a relief to get up and start a fire in the kitchen stove, grind beans for coffee, fry bacon.

Our city neighbors Theo and Joel also owned a house near us in the Catskills. They came over during breakfast to pick up Christopher and drive him back to the city.

Theo had offered to take care of Christopher all day. She attempted to be jovial, but it was too early in the morning. I hugged Chris good-bye and he whimpered, still sleepy. He trudged off into the snow with Theo and Joel, his favorite rag doll, "Fever," clutched to his chest.

Katherine, Philip, Jeremy, and I were silent, preoccupied, on the drive to Albany. A thin winter sun pierced through the gray sky, accentuating the still falling snow.

Jeffrey Laef, the attorney collaborating with Miriam, had mentioned our case a year or so earlier to an attorney friend during one of their routine bus rides to and from Albany. No one knew then that Nancy Hunt would be the first woman attorney to sit on the nine-member Court of Appeals. Jeffrey felt obligated to write Mrs. Hunt, reminding her of their conversation and informing her that we would be appearing before her court in February. She didn't respond, and we didn't know what, if anything, she would do about her prior knowledge.

We arrived in Albany early and sat in the courtroom listening to the cases on the roster before ours. Nancy Hunt was instantly recognizable amidst the sea of short-haired men behind the bench.

Schwartz walked into the courtroom. I felt my body stiffen as he looked directly at me. Something made me smile. Maybe it would unnerve him when he gave his oral argument.

Angelina appeared at the doorway. She scanned the gallery, found me, smiled expectantly. I looked away. I couldn't be friendly today. How did she get here, I wondered. With Schwartz? Did they talk?

When the clerk finally called out, "Rodriguez versus Ryan," Mrs. Hunt stood up and left the courtroom. She didn't return. So eight men listened to Miriam's argument. They weren't polite like the Appellate Division judges. They interrupted Miriam constantly, boring into her antagonistically.

We strained forward to hear clearly; the courtroom was large and the distance between the judges and us greater than in the lower courts. We couldn't even make out their features clearly. The black robes, the Latin phrases, the granite pillars of the courthouse were formal and forbidding.

We walked out of the courthouse into the dull darkening February air. On the long drive home to Manhattan, we tried to sort out what had happened. Katherine's legal training honed her analysis, and she tried to be optimistic, but Jeremy and I were glum.

"Chris, do you remember what adoption is?" The decision would come from Albany in the next week or so. I couldn't put this moment off any longer. We were sitting on Christopher's bed with a book; it was a quiet April afternoon.

"It's when you can't get a baby in your tummy. But you got the biggest baby in the whole nursery, and that was me." We'd been this far before, and Chris was satisfied; he liked to focus on his size at birth.

"Yes, but first you were in someone else's tummy."

Quickly, with great interest, came, "Whose?"

I took a deep breath. "Angelina's." I'd said it.

A little smile crossed his lips.

"How do you feel about that?"

"Happy." That's what he said. I wish he hadn't said happy, but he did. She'd probably been telling him that on Mondays. It might be reassuring to him, at almost four, to know that she was telling the truth.

Five minutes passed as we read. Then I said, "Chris, can we talk more about your having been in Angelina's tummy?"

His brown eyes, like saucers, locked into mine. "It makes me sad."

"Why?"

"Because I wanted to be in your tummy."

"That would have been good. I wanted that, too. But God didn't want me to have babies in my tummy."

"Why?"

"I don't know. I think he wanted me to wait for you."

"Yeah."

"You know Angelina wants you to live with her now."

"No. She can come on Monday and bring me toys."

"Well, you know, you were born in her tummy and that makes her your birth mother."

"But you're my mother."

"I'm your real mother. Angelina's your birth mother."

"I won't go with her. I always want to live with you and Dad."

"We always want you to live with us, too."

"Let's play with my cars."

I felt that I hadn't handled this conversation very well, but it was an opening. I told Dr. Eidelstein I needed more help. What if Angelina won? Could she appear at our house with a sheriff and a court order? Would she take Christopher straight to the airport to California? To El Salvador? It was unfair to him not to be prepared, unfair to Jeremy and me, unfair to everyone. It was time for Angelina and me to start talking. But we needed an arbiter and an interpreter and a neutral meeting ground without Christopher hovering about. Dr. Eidelstein suggested I contact Rosa Levano, a bilingual social worker under her supervision at Columbia Presbyterian's child psychiatric unit. Mrs. Levano set up a meeting with Angelina and me for the next Friday morning.

Angelina was already in the reception area when I arrived at Columbia Presbyterian. Mrs. Levano ushered us into her dimly lit office and invited us to be seated. Angelina chose the couch. It was small, loveseat size, so I sat in the armchair. I felt as if I'd been called into the principal's office to settle a squabble with a classmate.

But Mrs. Levano was gracious, easy to talk to, not intimidating at all. She spoke first to Angelina in Spanish, then to me in English. The language difference insulated me from Angelina and her from me. It kept a certain distance between us. And it was easier for me to be direct with Rosa, knowing that she could temper her Spanish translation for Angelina. I looked at Rosa when I spoke to her, not at Angelina. Angelina did the same. Rosa became our sounding board, our referee.

Rosa said it was important for Angelina and me each to know what the other was thinking. Angelina said she wanted me to know that she thought I had been a good mother to Christopher. She was aware of the depth of my feelings for him. If she won, she planned to take Christopher to California. We would be welcome to visit him there, she said.

Rosa said that there should be a transition period, a time for Christopher to get used to Angelina gradually, not all at once. We discussed outings for the two of them, or the three of us. I suggested Angelina and Chris start seeing New York together. There were so many wonderful excursions available, like the Metropolitan Museum, or the Bronx Zoo, or the South Street Seaport.

Angelina's world centered around the family for whom she worked on Fifth Avenue. Her main responsibility seemed to be escorting the little girl to and from various lessons and afterschool activities. Another full-time domestic had been with the family for fifteen years, and she did the heavy work, like laundry and washing floors. If the parents went out of town, the mother-in-law flew in, and she and Angelina were in charge of the children.

Maybe she could bring Christopher to Fifth Avenue overnight sometime, Angelina suggested.

Rosa stressed to her that it was Christopher who needed time. After spending his entire life with Jeremy and me, he might not be anxious to be with her. I related the conversation that Christopher and I had had about Angelina's wanting him to live with her. She seemed genuinely surprised that he wasn't excited about the prospect. I don't think it had begun to sink in for Angelina that to Christopher, *I* was Mom.

When Angelina and Rosa were talking, I could barely wait for the translation. At one point the door opened and three teenaged boys burst into Rosa's office. "How many times have I told you to knock?" Rosa said in exasperation. "My adolescents group," she apologized, "they have a meeting with me now." Our mood had been so intense, our scene so centered; none of us realized that we'd been talking for more than an hour.

At our next meeting with Rosa, Angelina mentioned that her employers would be out of town the following week. When I mentioned this to Theo, she said eagerly, "Why don't you go up there Monday? You can check out their apartment." So I proposed to Angelina that Christopher and I meet her at her apartment, then go out to lunch.

The following Monday, Angelina was waiting for us in the lobby. I looked hard at her, trying to read into those cool dark eyes. She was a pretty woman who looked much younger than thirty-five. It was partly her clothes—jeans, sweatshirts, boots; partly her hair—long, wavy, jet black, today tied at the crown with a piece of violet yarn; partly her demeanor—passive and obeisant.

"You wan going for lunch?" she asked Christopher.

"I thought we were going upstairs first," I said. I didn't

want to miss the grand tour. This was my chance to see how Angelina lived.

"Oh, my bed's not made," Angelina said.

"I promised Christopher we'd see your room," I said firmly.

"Oh, OK," said Angelina. "Chris, you wan see my room?"

The apartment was enormous and lovely. Perfect Upper East Side Taste and Money. We peeked briefly into all the rooms off a long marble foyer. A black, uniformed maid presided over one of two stoves in the kitchen. Angelina's room was wallpapered in provincial Pierre Deux; the adjoining bath gleamed with sleek navy tiles. I began feeling rather seedy.

"Mom," said Christopher, "when are we going to eat?"

Angelina seemed relieved to go out. I wondered if the maid would tell. I left reluctantly, looking back over my shoulder at the long, curved staircase leading to the second floor of the penthouse apartment with wraparound terrace on Fifth Avenue.

The elevator man and the doorman smiled fondly at Angelina. I wondered if they knew who Christopher was.

I suggested Jackson Hole, a nearby inexpensive hamburger restaurant.

"I want a cheeseburg," Christopher said.

"Me, too, cheeseburger," said Angelina.

"No," said Chris, "grilled cheese."

Angelina said, "OK, me too, grilled cheese."

"Chris," I asked, "would you like bacon on your grilled cheese?"

"Oh yeah, bacon, yum." He licked his upper lip.

Angelina said, "Me too, bacon."

"Three grilled cheese with bacon," I said to the waiter. I would have loved a hamburger, but it seemed gross next to a grilled cheese.

The decision came three days later. Morning rain had turned to afternoon sleet, then evening snow. It was unanimous against us—eight to zero. Miriam and Jeffrey did not recommend our appealing to the United States Supreme Court in Washington, which was even more conservative than the Court of Appeals.

Angelina and I were in Rosa's office the next morning for our weekly appointment. She seemed as calm and nonchalant as ever. Her plan was to stay with her employers on Fifth Avenue until June, when their children would be out of school. I was amazed that her decision was based on her employer's children rather than on Christopher.

So we had until June. Angelina would speak with her employer about having Christopher spend Sunday nights with her on Fifth Avenue. She would write her California attorney about schools for the fall. We three sat so calmly, rationally, as if we were planning a dinner party. As Rosa and Angelina spoke in Spanish, I thought to myself, "I don't believe it. What if I told her she has to take him now, not when those kids finish school?" But I didn't react that way. I, too, was calm, polite, controlled. No matter how furious I was with Angelina, I wanted Christopher, and I wanted her to let me keep him for as long as possible.

Christopher went with me to meet Rosa a few days later. I brought along a book we'd been given, *Why Was I Adopted?*, which explains the facts of adoption "with love and illustrations." It's a straightforward, thorough book that presents birth parents positively: "Every single baby had a mother and father. That mother and father gave you a very special gift. It's so special that no one else can ever give it to you and so special that even they can give it to you only once. They gave you the gift of life. By giving you the gift of life, they gave you your birthday."

Adoptive parents are introduced like this: "If you are an adopted child, you became part of your family in a different way than by just being born into it. You were wanted by somebody very, very much. They wanted *you!* (Not a bad choice. They must be pretty smart.)"

The book warns adopted children about not getting stuck up just because they're special: "You still have to go to bed when you're told and brush your teeth and eat your spinach and carrots."

Not all was sweetness and light when we read this book. Once Christopher intentionally ripped the book's jacket. I wanted to proceed gently. There is just so much a four-year-old can absorb.

The following Monday morning Christopher accompanied me to my appointment with Rosa and Angelina. During the trial, Schwartz had said Angelina would be allowed to bring Christopher to the Lieberman's "eleven-room duplex penthouse" to stay overnight on Sundays. This morning Angelina reported that Mrs. Lieberman had changed her mind; it would be too disruptive to have Christopher in their house.

Chris, Angelina, and I took the bus to Central Park after the appointment. I was angry with the Liebermans. My child wasn't good enough for them? I didn't feel like talking with Angelina. She picked up my mood and strayed to the other side of the playground. Chris played in the tunnels, ran across the bridges. Angelina and I both wore long black coats. Hers was down, mine, wool. We looked like guards for this child, staking out our turf on opposite benches. It was a cold, raw day. Christopher was hungry, so I bought him a hot dog from a stand. Angelina wrinkled her nose at the hot dogs. I told her that Christopher and I liked them just fine.

The next Monday I let Angelina take Christopher out alone for the first time. They lunched at McDonald's, a block away, and were home in half an hour. So much for discovering New York.

Norman called that evening. The college student in Colorado had given birth and was going to keep the child. We told him we wanted our money back. He'd see what he could do.

A few days later, Stanley's new associate called to say she had a surefire prospect for us, a baby to be born on the Fourth of July. "I don't know if I can stand to be burned again," I said wearily to Jeremy. We said yes, but put up no money in advance.

CHAPTER

Fourteen

On Easter morning, Christopher awoke primed for the hunt. He ran squealing from egg to egg, wearing his red flannel pajamas with the flap in the back.

Angelina arrived right on time. We were all going to the bilingual Mass, then Angelina was taking Christopher overnight to her friend's apartment in the Bronx for the first time—my idea. We were now in a "transition period," though I'm not sure any of us knew what that meant. Whose transition was it, anyway?

I had packed Chris's nylon flight bag with great care. Along with clothing and a toothbrush, I put in three new books, in Spanish with English translations: *500 Words to Grow On; The Four Seasons;* and *Big Dog, Little Dog.* Christopher often asked Angelina to read to him, but I never heard any reading. These books might help.

Christopher held both our hands as Angelina and I walked him around the block to church. Jeremy said he would meet us there. I don't think he could bear to walk in with Angelina.

I had chosen Christopher's outfit carefully, imagining Angelina's scrutiny once she had him all to herself, out of our house for the first time. A white shirt with red piping on the Peter Pan collar, navy wool pants, and a matching navy crewneck with red, yellow, and green stitching across the chest. Christopher looked adorable, especially with a smear of chocolate bunny across his lips.

Two days earlier, on Good Friday, I'd left Christopher napping with a neighbor while I went to church for *Tre Ore*. Representing the three hours after Christ is nailed to the cross before He dies, this service is staggeringly powerful in its starkness. I slipped into a pew at the rear of the packed church and was riveted to the soloist's plaintive wail, "My God, My God, why have You abandoned me?" Christ had cried out to His father, so alone, so humanly hopeless at that moment. I felt numb. Had God abandoned me, too?

Way up in the front of the church, I recognized Angelina's gray tweed coat and her long dark hair. She came to our church, I thought. She wants to be more a part of our lives; to see what church will be like here on Easter. She understands. She loves Jesus as I do. He forgives. Just before He dies on the cross, He forgives His murderers: "Father, forgive them, for they know not what they do."

I couldn't take my eyes off Angelina's back, waiting for her to turn and see me. I felt released. Tears rolled down my cheeks. I had been blessed with the power to forgive. She did what she had to do. I can forgive her. We are loving our son.

The gray coat wasn't Angelina. But a catharsis had occurred. In a graced moment, my emotions had been mined, and I felt free.

The feeling was shortlived. Back in church on Easter Sunday, now with Christopher, Jeremy, and Angelina, the triumphal resurrection of Christ was far from my mind. My stomach was in knots in anticipation of Christopher's first overnight away from us in his three and three-quarters years of life. When Angelina and I went up the middle aisle to receive communion, Christopher scurried behind us. "Mom, I want a piece of bread."

"No, Chris, not until you're seven." How can you tell a three-year-old, "You can have a piece of bread when you reach the age of reason." I usually gave him a cracker at communion, but today I'd forgotten the cracker.

When Father Patrick said, "Let us offer each other a sign of peace," Angelina and I shook hands. I knew her handshake would be limp. She offered her hand to Jeremy; he didn't take it. He left church just before the service ended.

Back at the loft after church, Christopher swung from his gym rings. Jeremy and I had debated for two weeks, then accepted our annual invitation from friends in Connecticut for Easter dinner. I figured we'd just feel worse if we sat at home.

It was time for us to leave. Angelina sat watching Christopher on his rings. She hadn't said a word since church. She seldom spoke when Jeremy was home.

I said, "Okay, Chris, time to go."

Christopher twirled on the rings and said, "Not yet."

I said, "Chris, I mean it. Let go of the rings."

"No way."

I tried to take his hands from the rings. He tightened his grip. Angelina watched.

Jeremy said, "Christopher."

"I'm not going."

"Come on, Chris," Angelina murmured, "we get candy."

"NO!"

I peeled his fingers one by one from the rings. His knuckles were white. He started screaming and ran down the loft's central hallway toward the living room.

"Christopher," Jeremy said, going after him. "I'm sorry. I don't want you to go. Mom doesn't want you to go. But you have to go. Come on. You'll have fun."

Christopher turned the TV on.

"Christopher! Jeremy, I need some help here," I said.

"Okay, Chris, let's go," said Jeremy, clapping his hands, "get in the elevator."

Angelina picked up the flight bag. I pressed the down button. Jeremy picked up Christopher and carried him into the elevator. His screams got louder and louder. He thrashed around in Jeremy's arms, almost knocking him down.

"Jeremy, let's go down with them," I said. "I can't let him go like this."

In the lobby, Christopher ran to the corner near the basement door. "I won't," he screamed, "I won't."

"Jeremy, let's drive them to the Bronx," I said. "I'm not letting him go down the street like this."

"I don't think it's a good idea," said Jeremy.

"I can't let him go like this."

Angelina frowned. "I wan going Fifth Avenue," she said. "I get my coat first."

"Okay," sighed Jeremy, "the car is right outside."

Jeremy drove. Angelina got in the back. I held Christopher on my lap in the front. He sobbed and sobbed, his face buried in my shoulder. My hair was wet from his tears.

"I don't want to go, Mom," he said over and over.

"I know, honey," I said. "I'm sorry, you have to go."

"Please don't make me go, Mom."

"It's just for one night, Chris. You'll be home tomorrow."

"Please, Mom."

We headed north on the FDR drive. Jeremy drove very fast. The sun was pale and cool.

When Jeremy stopped the car on Fifth Avenue, Chris's crying turned to screaming again.

"Good-bye, love," I hugged Christopher. "You call me. Here's Katy and Tom's number." I tucked the paper into the pocket of his Yankees jacket.

"Please, Mom," he whimpered.

I shut the door. "Let's go," I said to Jeremy. "Fast."

In Connecticut, no one mentioned Christopher. I finally started talking about him just to convince myself that he was alive.

We got home again at about nine o'clock. A few minutes later the phone rang.

"Hi, Mom, I'm at Angelina's friend's house. We're watching *King Kong* on TV."

"Christopher. Oh, baby, I'm so glad you called. Did you have dinner?"

"Yeah, macaroni and cheese. And chicken. It was real good."

"Good. I'm *so* glad you called. I love you, honey."

"Me too. Mom, did you ever see *King Kong*?"

"I'm not sure. Is it scary?"

"A tiny bit. Is Daddy there?"

"Dad, did you ever see *King Kong*?" he said when I put Jeremy on.

"Yes, Chris, isn't it great?"

"Dad, I called lots of times. Where were you?"

"Remember, Chris, we went to Katy and Tom's."

"Dad, next time I want to go to Katy and Tom's."

"Okay, Chris, you will. I'm going to say good-night now, OK? I love you."

Christopher called six or seven more times during the

next half-hour. His calls got increasingly silly. He was all right.

I woke with a start, my wet nightgown clinging to me. King Kong had been chasing Chris and me. Jeremy had already left for work.

Christopher and Angelina weren't expected back until 6:00 P.M. My book club was meeting that night; I decided to spend the rainy day in bed with *The Name of the Rose.* After an hour or so, I could feel the quiet.

The buzzer rang at eleven. Angelina and Christopher stepped out of the elevator dripping wet. I was embarrassed to be caught in my bathrobe.

"Chris wan coming home," said Angelina.

"Hi, Mom," said Christopher casually. "I had toast in a restaurant."

"You're lucky I'm here," I said. But then I'm always here, I thought.

"Chris no have boots and he wan coming home," said Angelina.

Now that they were finally back, I was disappointed to lose my reading day. "Okay, Chris, let's get your boots. Where are you guys going for lunch?"

"Grilled cheese at home," said Christopher.

"Chris, wan go McDonald's?" asked Angelina.

"Home."

"How about Chinese?" I said. "Spareribs, Chris? The one down the block?"

"I *said*," Christopher announced emphatically, "grilled cheese at home."

I sighed. Thank God Angelina has the sense to come in out of the rain.

Christopher didn't have much to say about his overnight with Angelina, only that no one was home when they arrived in the Bronx and that they had had to wait on the Cabas's porch. There was something hanging on the wall in the apartment, "like a big statue," that scared him and kept him from getting to sleep that night. *King Kong* would not have been my choice for a bedtime movie. I hated the thought of his having been in the South Bronx, with its rundown tenements, drug dealers, broken windows, broken dreams. I hated not knowing everything that had happened since we'd dropped him off the morning before.

For Mother's Day, Angelina and I had arranged that she would pick up Christopher at my church soup kitchen, where I worked on Sunday mornings when we stayed in the city for the weekend. Chris was playing tag with another child in the dining hall and I was rinsing heads of lettuce in the sink when Angelina appeared in the kitchen doorway, clutching a cone of florist's paper in her hand. She extended it to me and I tore open the paper, exposing a bunch of baby's breath encircling a single red rose. Pretty, understated. It hadn't occurred to me to buy her a gift for Mother's Day. When Christopher saw her, he ran to me and clung to my skirt, whimpering, "Mom, I don't want to go with her. Please, Mom."

"Christopher," I said, "stop crying. You have to go." A few women chopping vegetables looked at us with interest, sensing a drama. I had hoped that departing from a public place instead of our home would be easier. Chris enjoyed being with Angelina, but he was frightened about going off with her.

Leaving Christopher to trail behind me, I walked out of the kitchen and over to Angelina, now chatting in Spanish with Father Patrick and Sister Marianne. "*You* have to take him," I said. "I can't make him go." I turned and walked back into the kitchen.

Angelina tried to hoist Chris up on her hip, but he bucked back, crying. He was too big to be carried by such a little woman. I was embarrassed and angry, blowing puffs of air out between pursed lips as I hacked away at carrots for the soup. The woman working next to me said, "Put the knife down. Take a deep breath. Let all the air collect in your head. Count to ten slowly. Let the air out." I had to leave. I gave Sister Marianne the flowers.

I met Jeremy and friends at a local restaurant for brunch. Everyone toasted me for Mother's Day, which seemed absurd. Both Jeremy and I drank too much wine. Later, at home, I yelled at him, "I can't do this by myself."

"You're the one that wanted to go to the soup kitchen," he said. "I didn't make you go."

"Forget it," I said. "I'm going to bed." I awoke about three in the morning with a terrific headache and couldn't get back to sleep the rest of the night. Angelina had been allowed to bring Christopher overnight to Fifth Avenue.

Dr. Eidelstein had asked to see Christopher at our next appointment with Rosa Levano. Angelina brought him from Fifth Avenue with her, so he hadn't seen me since we parted ways in the soup kitchen the morning before. I wondered if our separation would have any effect on what he said to "Dr. E," our name for Dr. Eidelstein. What Chris remembered about having met with her the previous summer was that she lived across the street from the Museum of Natural History and we went to see the dinosaurs after our appointment.

Christopher was already alone with Dr. Eidelstein when I arrived. Angelina and I waited with Rosa. Angelina told us that Chris had kicked her when she tried to make him take his pants down to go to the bathroom the night before. I was pleased with Christopher for kicking Angelina, but my face remained impassive.

Christopher and Dr. E appeared in Rosa's doorway. He looked so serious, so sweet. He beamed when he saw me.

Dr. E sat in the extra chair, so Chris was squished in between Angelina and me on the loveseat. He held my hand. Dr. E told us that Christopher had told her he knew what adoption was. He was in Angelina's stomach. She was his birth mother. Mom was his real mother. No, he didn't want to live with Angelina. He wanted to live with Mom and Dad forever.

Dr. E said it was important that the transition be gradual, taking perhaps as long as a year. Angelina listened carefully to Rosa's translation, her forehead furrowed in concentration. Dr. E talked about the regression that could occur and what we should all watch for—loss of appetite, loss of toilet training, temper tantrums.

Although he was scheduled to spend the rest of the afternoon with Angelina, Christopher wanted to come with me after the appointment. I had a lunch date with Miriam Friedman, our attorney. "I just want to *see* Miriam," he said. So Angelina, Christopher, and I trooped down to Columbia Law School. Miriam looked stunned to see Angelina. She was used to dealing with her in the abstract, in a brief. The opposition in the flesh must have been quite a surprise. Chris seemed satisfied to have seen Miriam, and he agreed to leave with Angelina, "*if* we go to McDonald's."

"I'll be home at four, Mom," he said. "All right? Four o'clock." He was running the show.

Angelina showed up halfway through our next appointment with Rosa Levano. Usually she dressed well for these visits, but today she wore faded jeans and an old sweatshirt. Her hair was dull, unwashed, pulled back with an elastic band into a ponytail. Her eyes were swollen. She said she was having trouble sleeping, she felt nauseous, she had had headaches. She sat tensely on the edge of her chair, twisting her hands together. Suddenly she stood up and said, "I have to go home. I can't stay. I am sorry." And she left the room.

"I'm not surprised at this behavior," said Rosa. "As a matter of fact, I've been anticipating it."

"Is this illness psychosomatic?" I asked.

"I think so," said Rosa. "The prospect of taking Christopher away, of having ultimate responsibility for him, could be making her sick with anxiety. She said she had to get back to work, but she took the time to come up here. She could have just phoned to cancel. I think she wanted to touch base with us, but then she simply couldn't stand to stay. Let's give her time to get home. Then I'll call her to make sure she's all right."

"I wanted to talk with you alone, anyway," said Rosa. "I wonder what *Mr.* Ryan has to say? Do you think he might like to meet with us?"

"I doubt it," I said. "Jeremy is suspicious of social workers, leery of anything psychological. I think he views it as weakness."

"A lot of men do," said Rosa. "As a defense. But this issue is complicated. He may not be able to open up as easily as you."

"Frankly, Rosa, I'd just like to leave him out of it," I said. "I think Angelina is afraid of him. It might intimidate her if he came here with me."

"I asked Angelina how she felt about you," Rosa said. "She said she felt you did what you had to do, she isn't angry with you. But she said Mr. Ryan is not nice to her."

"He's *not* nice to her," I admitted. I'd never seen Jeremy treat anyone the way he treated Angelina. Basically he ignored her. "He can't forgive her," I said. "He's still very angry with Angelina, and it's hard for him to even have her around." I wanted Angelina to know

Jeremy was a loving husband and a good father. His grievances were imprisoning him.

"Maybe Mr. Ryan will join us later on," said Rosa. "He's going to need to talk about this."

I nodded, deciding not to mention my frustration with Jeremy's avoidance of discussing anything unpleasant. He had no interest in participating with Angelina and Rosa in these sessions. When he had gone to see Dr. Eidelstein with me, he hadn't said much. Like most men, he found it difficult to open up about feelings.

Over the years he'd conditioned himself to suppress or deny any feelings that became too negative or complicated. Dr. Eidelstein had suggested I listen very carefully to Jeremy. That made me stop: Carla, the therapist I'd seen a few years earlier, had told me the same thing.

I began praying for Jeremy and me at different times during the day, not on my knees, but when weeding the garden, or taking a shower. I asked God for the grace to be with Jeremy and me when we were talking about Angelina.

Rosa phoned Angelina, who apologized for her abrupt departure and said she was working too hard. She would go to see a doctor about her headaches. She'd try to get more sleep. I'm sure Angelina wasn't particularly comfortable dealing with a social worker, either. As a domestic employed by upper-class people, she'd probably grown used to concealing her true feelings. She probably didn't have enough sophistication to realize her illness was psychosomatic.

Angelina told Rosa she'd like to come to the Catskills with us some weekend soon. She might not leave for California in June.

The next Monday I invited Angelina to join us at the Cooper Hewitt Museum garden party. She lived close to the museum, so it seemed natural enough for her to stop by the party on her way home from visiting us.

Christopher wanted some ginger ale, so we walked across the lawn to the bar. A string quartet played Scarlatti in the center of the grassy rectangular yard—three tuxedoed men and a red-haired woman in a lavender dress. Elderly women whispered together on wrought iron benches. Pink and purple impatiens trembled in the June breeze.

Christopher stood between Angelina and me. He was wearing a pinstriped sunsuit and sandals. One hand held the plastic glass of ginger ale; the other hand was filled with pretzels. He raised the whole fistful up to his mouth so he could still hold the ginger ale. Most of the pretzels fell on the manicured grass. Angelina was drinking ginger ale, too. She always had whatever Christopher had. I sipped my white wine and squinted into the sun.

A straw-hatted dowager toddled by and beamed down at Christopher. A nosegay of fresh violets was pinned on the bosom of her voile dress.

"What a beautiful child," her voice quavered. "He's lovely."

Angelina and I nodded in assent.

"How old is he?"

"He's three," we both said.

"He'll be four next month," I clarified.

"Well," she said, looking back and forth from Angelina to me. "Which one is the mother? Is it you?" she finally said to Angelina.

"Yes," Angelina replied.

I felt a lump in my throat. It was difficult to keep smiling. I decided not to say anything.

"Well," said Angelina, looking at me, "she is the mother, too. We are both the mother."

The old woman looked at Angelina carefully, then

turned to me and said, "Does he eat well? Does he like vegetables?"

A wave of tenderness for Angelina washed over me. I looked at her and said, smiling, "Oh, come on, why don't you have some wine?"

CHAPTER
Fifteen

When we came home from the Catskills the following Sunday evening, I rewound the answering machine. Arlene Feinman, Norman's replacement, had called earlier that day. I decided to call her the next morning and proceeded with our frequent Sunday night return-from-the-country plan of action—ordering Chinese food for dinner.

Christopher was in the bathtub when Arlene called again.

"Maggie. Congratulations on your new son."

I almost said, "But we just ordered Chinese." What I did say was, "Omigod. I thought the baby wasn't due until the Fourth of July" (three weeks away).

"Well, he was born this morning," said Arlene, "a beautiful little boy. Seven pounds exactly."

"A boy," I said dully, echoing Arlene.

"Yes, you knew he was going to be a boy. That's what the sonogram showed."

"Oh, right," I said. I'd decided to be offhand about this

possible baby and hadn't bothered to research the sexual accuracy of a sonogram.

"He's just fine," chirped Arlene.

"When can we see him?" I asked.

"We'll talk again tomorrow," she said. "I just wanted you to know right away. Congratulations again." She rang off.

I slumped against the kitchen wall, my hand patting my chest. No physical or emotional preparation; no advance notice.

Jeremy came upstairs from parking the car. "Guess what?" I said. "We're a family." I'd always thought that having one child meant you were a couple with a child. With two children, you became a family.

We decided not to tell Christopher about the baby until the consent was signed and we were assured that everything was as secure as could be.

I phoned Arlene the next morning. The baby was jaundiced, she said, and would have to stay at the hospital a few days more. No, we couldn't visit him. We couldn't talk with the doctors. Her office had already sent flowers to the birth mother. There was nothing for us to do but wait.

By Wednesday I was incredibly anxious, largely because we were supposed to leave on Friday at noon for the Catskills weekend with Angelina.

"Why can't we talk with the doctor?" I demanded of Arlene. "Is it simply jaundice or something more? Christopher was jaundiced too, but he left the hospital when he was two days old."

"You'll just have to wait," Arlene said. "The doctor knows what's best for the baby."

"But we have plans to leave the city Friday," I persisted. "Chris's biological mother is coming with us to the country for the weekend. I don't want to mess things up with her."

"Maggie," said Arlene, "maybe you and Jeremy aren't ready for another baby yet. Maybe you'd better wait until you straighten things out with Christopher."

"We are ready for this baby, Arlene," I said, trying to keep the anger out of my tone. "I just don't think it's necessary to keep a baby in the hospital for five days. And we haven't even seen him yet. He could be bonded to me by now. All babies are jaundiced to some degree; that's what Chris's doctor told us. Their livers haven't kicked in yet."

"Maggie, I don't believe this. I've never had a client try to tell a doctor what to do. I don't think you can coordinate your weekend plans, whatever they are, with the arrival of a new baby."

A cold fear crept over me. I realized my stupidity, telling Arlene about Christopher and Angelina. By showing my concern about Angelina, I was seriously endangering our chances for number two.

The next day I came to understand for the first time the expression *beside myself*. I was not sure what I was doing. Christopher's fourth birthday was coming up, and I tried to concentrate on sending out invitations. A friend later told me the invitation he'd received was blank; luckily he'd recognized my handwriting on the envelope. Why didn't Arlene call? In mid-afternoon I phoned Angelina and told her we'd be leaving Saturday morning instead of Friday. "Something came up," I said. No problem.

Friday morning. Waiting. Christopher was out of school for the summer and was happily entrenched in his rocker watching "Sesame Street" on television when the phone rang. I bolted to answer, saying out loud, "At last." It was my cousin Eva. I hadn't heard from her in years, only about her from my mother—that she was teaching English in a small college upstate, that she had a baby. Her call today was to inquire about whether she could come to the Catskills for several days. She had decided to break up with the father of her child and had given him a week's notice to pack up his stuff and get out. When I told her about the new baby, she still wanted to know if she could come. Why not, I thought. The more, the merrier. On the other hand, her single-mother status might give Angelina some ideas. Then again, it might help to have somebody else around to deflect any tension between Angelina and Jeremy. I'd never seen Eva's son, Max, and was intrigued with the notion of her being a mother. She'd done graduate work in Germany, doctoral studies in Japan, and had bounced around California for years before "settling" in upstate New York.

When I hung up on Eva, Arlene called. She said to be at her office in New Hyde Park by noon. She would accompany us to the hospital to pick up the baby. I sat down with Christopher and told him we had a big surprise for him. We were going to adopt a new baby that was five days old. The baby was waiting for us to come and pick him up at the hospital. "Can I go?" were Chris's first words.

"Theo wants you to come up and wait with her," I said. "Daddy and I might have to wait at the hospital for a while, and I think you'd have more fun at Theo's."

"OK," he sighed in a resigned way.

"The second we get home we'll come up to Theo's to get you. You'll be a big brother." Chris beamed. "Where will he sleep?" He looked around as if a bed might materialize.

"In your same old bassinet," I said.

He looked relieved. "Because he could fall out of my bed now that the sides are down," he said.

Arlene told us to wait in the car while she went into the hospital to get Will. We didn't park the car; we stayed at the curbside where we'd pulled up to drop off Arlene. "This sure is different from San Francisco General," I said to Jeremy, referring to our hospital experience with Christopher.

"If it makes the hospital feel better by not letting us in, there's not a lot we can do about it," he said.

"But it's weird to wait for a baby in the parking lot," I said. Arlene had seemed upset that I hadn't brought an undershirt for Will. All I had brought along was an old kimono of Christopher's and a receiving blanket. I hadn't bought any new baby clothes.

"What's taking them so long?" I said after about thirty minutes. It was a hot June day. For good luck, I wore the same outfit I'd worn in San Francisco four years earlier to pick up Christopher. That day I'd felt so up, but today I felt wearier, worn, apprehensive. The revolving doors kept going around. A steady stream of healthy-looking people, people in wheelchairs, children, came through the hospital doors. The wait was unbearable.

Suddenly Arlene appeared next to a nurse in a white dress who wheeled a tall box over to the curb. The nurse handed the bundle to Arlene, who handed it to me in the backseat. I peered in at the swaddled baby. He was sleeping. His skin was tawny, golden, suntanned. "Look," I whispered to Jeremy, "he's gorgeous."

Jeremy went up to Theo's to bring Christopher down. He sat on the couch, and I put Will on his lap. Chris ran a finger along the baby's cheek, and Will's eyes opened for the first time. They were bright blue. I unwrapped his receiving blanket. His head was bald. "He looks like a Cabbage Patch Kid," said Christopher.

"When you were a new baby," I told Chris, "your hair stood straight up, just like a punk rocker."

Chris giggled. "Maybe his will grow," he said hopefully.

We counted Will's fingers and toes together.

"I can help take care of him," Chris offered.

"That will be great," I said. "I think I'm going to need your help."

Jeremy and I had felt Christopher should meet Will first, but I knew Theo was dying to come down. Jeremy phoned her and she appeared in seconds. As she cradled Will against her cheek, Theo pointed out that Chris's olive complexion and mine were similar, while Will's paler coloring was just like Jeremy's.

"One of the real sorrows of my life is that I've never been a godmother," said Theo. Jeremy and I looked at each other and burst out laughing.

"I have a feeling you're about to become one," Jeremy said.

"A fairy godmother?" asked Chris, incredulous. We all laughed this time, and as I looked into the enormous mirror opposite the couch we sat on, I thought we looked happy and complete, a cozy little family and their fairy godmother.

The next morning rain poured, an incredibly heavy thunderstorm. When the doorbell buzzed, I told Christopher to greet Angelina at the elevator and bring her to the living room, saying we had a surprise. I sat in the rocker holding Will, practicing smiles, bracing myself. Angelina walked into the room, saw us in the corner, and covered her mouth with her hand. "Oh, my God," she said. Her big eyes seemed to grow. She had probably thought the surprise would be new draperies or a couch.

"Hi," I said. "This is our new baby."

"Is boy or girl?" she asked.

"A boy," I said, "Will."

"Will," she echoed. "Adopted?"

"Yes."

"How old is baby?"

"Five days."

"Oh, my God," she said. "Beautiful baby. Can I hold him?" And Angelina sat rocking Will while I finished packing for the country. "I don believe it," she murmured over and over.

"Poor baby," I said to Jeremy as we headed up the thruway. "He doesn't even get to spend his first weekend at home."

"That's not true," said Jeremy. "He's just spending it at his country home instead of his city home. I think he's pretty lucky."

Cousin Eva and nephew Max showed up about an hour after we arrived in the Catskills. Eva proved to be resourceful, inviting Angelina to help her weed the stone patio, offering Angelina a baby wipe when our water supply (a garden hose hooked up to the spring across the river) got washed out in the heavy rains. Angelina sat in an old wicker rocker on the porch with Will in her arms. "I like babies," I heard her tell Eva, "but no married."

"Well," began Eva, but I shot her a warning look. "It could be difficult," she finished weakly.

Jeremy, Angelina, Christopher, Eva, and Max went to the local auction that night, leaving me at home with Will. On Sunday it poured again, so I took Chris and Angelina out for pizza, leaving the others at home. I felt obligated to entertain Angelina, who probably would have been just as happy staying at the house.

Jeremy was driving back to the city early Monday

morning; he would give Angelina a ride. She came into our bedroom to say good-bye. Chris and Will were both in bed with me. I'm sure it was difficult for her to tear herself away from this scene, particularly with the prospect of spending the next three hours in a small car with a hostile driver. I told Angelina that Christopher and I had already done some birthday party shopping at Woolworth's—he'd chosen plates, cups, and napkins featuring He-Man, the cartoon idol of little boys. I suggested that she order an ice cream cake from Carvel's with a He-Man decoration on the top. The boys and I would return to the city in two weeks for Christopher's party and Will's baptism.

On the phone that night, I asked Jeremy what he and Angelina had talked about on their ride to the city. "Nothing," he replied.

"Nothing in three hours? Not one word?" I asked incredulously.

"Well," he allowed, "after I parked the car and walked toward the house, she came after me mumbling something about a paper plate. She came upstairs with me to pick up a He-Man plate."

The vision of Angelina and Jeremy riding along in stony silence made me feel sorry for both of them. I could imagine Jeremy driving too fast in his rush to get home and Angelina cowering, leaning toward the door on the passenger side. Jeremy probably figured, What was there to talk with her about? Why bother to make small talk? To be fair to Jeremy, it was a simple fact that Angelina didn't speak much English. It would have been difficult to carry on a real conversation with her.

I'm sure it never occurred to Jeremy to drive her home to Fifth Avenue. He probably didn't even say good-bye to her, just turned and walked down the street. Angelina, "knowing her place," wouldn't dare to open her mouth unless he talked first. But she got her He-Man plate.

Maybe I projected too much for both Jeremy and Angelina. Maybe neither of them had any more feelings than the ones they showed. My husband and our son's birth mother made a strange couple indeed.

Jeremy is an intensely private man. It seems to me that unless he keeps a certain guard around himself, he might let go completely. His anger with Angelina remained one-dimensional, continuous, without shading or nuances.

Jeremy and I were surviving separately, distanced, polarized. I was dealing with Angelina while he ignored her. While this angered me, I felt strong, able. We didn't have to be welded together, after all. We each did what we could.

Angelina was a human being, just like the rest of us. She didn't seem to have an evil bone in her. My interpretation of her conduct at this point was that she had relied on the biological father to marry her when faced with the alternative of an adoption. It hadn't worked (little did she know that he already had two children and hadn't married *their* mother). Later the father's sister encouraged Angelina to fight. Angelina was passive, susceptible to any strong influence around her. Though I would never fully understand her behavior, I was beginning to separate it as something apart from her. The wrong had been done. The past could not be changed. Angelina wasn't going to go away. Where, after all, did she have to go? Back to San Francisco, where the biological father had finally married someone else? Back to El Salvador, where bombing had become a way of life? Maybe Angelina truly did love Christopher. She said she wanted him to be happy. If his being happy meant not being with her, then she would wait.

Rosa Levano had once asked Angelina if she was involved with any men in New York. "Well," Angelina allowed, "there are some people from El Salvador that live on Long Island. My sister sent me their address. One man there, Ramon, is interested in me." But Rosa told me that Angelina didn't want me to think of her as tainted in any way. She wanted to look good in my eyes.

Angelina took a taxi so that the He-Man ice cream cake wouldn't melt. Friends of various ages came to the party, including a colleague of mine from my former job, a man in his early sixties. The letter he wrote a few days later read:

> Christopher's birthday party for me became a celebration of life. It made me palpably aware—perhaps for the first time in my life—that God does indeed move in mysterious ways. You and Jeremy have so much love to give, and it happens to be love that is given in the only meaningful ways that matter. And so you know who the real beneficiaries are besides Christopher and Will? Me—and all of us whose lives were fortunate to be touched by yours in such a wonderful way.
>
> And so I celebrate not only the continuing wonder of Christopher but also the miracle of little Will. May God continue to be an integral part of your very loving lives.
>
> I pray that Angelina's life takes on significant meaning and beauty because of what you have contributed to it.

"Where will I sleep?" asked Angelina when she arrived for her two-week vacation in the Catskills. Maybe she hoped to share Christopher's room, with its austere, iron-frame, decidedly single bed. Will slept in a bassinet in Jeremy's and my room. My mother, with us for August, slept on the living room couch, because I was afraid to have her climbing the rickety stairs when she got up at night to go to the bathroom. I gave Angelina the guest room.

Will and I are the first ones up in the morning. I rattle around the kitchen in my red flannel nightgown and slipper socks, wadding up old copies of the *Catskill Mountain News* to start a fire in the wood stove, warming Will's formula, making coffee. Will tracks me from his rocking recliner, gurgling, a happy baby. It is cool in the morning before the sun comes up, and Will wears an off-white, hand-crocheted cap tied under his chin, masking his baldness, giving him an old-fashioned look. A mohair blanket is tucked around him, but he keeps kicking it off with his booties. "You are my sunshine, my only sunshine, you make me happy when skies are gray," I sing to him, just as my mother, not yet up this morning, sang to me when I was a baby. A Paddington Bear mobile dangles from one of the wood ceiling rafters, and Will never seems to tire of watching the blue-coated bears go bobbing around and around in their yellow hats and red boots.

I can prop up Will's bottle with one arm and drink my coffee with my free hand. Below the white wainscoting, the kitchen wallpaper is bottle green with tiny lavender diamonds. The paper above the railing is white with lavender buds and green stems, a design that looks abstract until you're about a foot in front of it. Just below the ceiling is a stencilled border of Shakerlike deep red hearts. Jeremy had surprised me by proposing these three different patterns; he usually prefers something purer, more high tech. This paper was a sweet side of him, I decided. Our country existence was a dramatic counterpoint to city life. And Jeremy was back in the sticky city, probably at his office already, working hard to support this idyll.

As I sit feeding Will, musing about Jeremy, Angelina appears, yawning good-morning, her long black hair flowing over the shoulders of her white terrycloth robe. By now the fog has lifted from the mountains and the sun is warm on the porch outside the kitchen. We sit in wicker rocking chairs drinking coffee, one of us occasionally sticking a foot out to rock Will's recliner, now on the porch floor.

We don't have much to talk about beyond the kids, the local produce, the weather. I ask questions about her family, life in El Salvador, but her answers are monosyllabic, not conducive to real conversation. When my mother and Chris wander into the kitchen an hour or so later, we're busy with breakfast. Christopher and Angelina disappear to play—in the sandbox, or down by the river, or behind the clump of spruce trees.

My mother and Angelina became confidantes of sorts. They are similar women—simple, uncomplicated, naive, dependent, gentle. Angelina told my mother that she had a boyfriend who wanted to marry her. He had been married before but divorced his wife because she couldn't have children. My mother also reported that she heard Angelina ask Christopher if he wanted to take the bus back to the city with her. His response was "no."

Angelina didn't mention this to me, and I was terrified that she might propose taking him back with her. Should I say something to her or wait until she approaches me? Days passed and she said nothing. It occurred to me that she might mention certain things in front of my mother as a kind of test, knowing that my mother would report to me. Or maybe I was complicating things. Maybe she sensed a kindred spirit in my mother and was looking for support. Or maybe none of these. My mind spun, my guesses unconfirmed.

One day I packed a picnic lunch and we all piled into the car to drive to a state forest pond about thirty minutes away. First I dropped off several sacks of dirty clothes at the laundry, telling the manager I'd be back to pick everything up before the 4:30 closing. While Will and my mother napped in the shade, Christopher, Angelina, and I swam. We had a lovely afternoon and pulled up in front of the laundromat about ten minutes before closing. The door was locked.

"Oh, this watch," sighed my mother, "it's always a half-hour slow."

"Mother, if it's always a half-hour slow, why didn't you tell me that? We have no sheets for the beds, no towels, no clean clothes for the kids." My mother looked like she might cry.

"Never mind," I said. I decided to take everyone to the local Chinese restaurant, then to the movie in town. Will was fussing, squirming. Christopher ordered spareribs. Angelina, of course, ordered spareribs too. I ordered a beer, but the restaurant didn't have a liquor license. Will cried so loud that I took him outside, telling my mother to order for me. When I came back in, she'd ordered chow mein, the one Chinese dish I loathe. "Forget it," I said, "let's just go to the movie. It starts in ten minutes."

"Oh, dear, I'm afraid my watch is slow again," said my mother.

I told everybody to get in the car and ordered two egg rolls to go. We drove home. I put Will in bed and downed two vodka and tonics with my egg rolls. I felt much better to have done something just for me, not taking care of my mother, Angelina, Chris, and Will, my "four children," as I complained to Jeremy on the phone. I envied his city solitude.

Jeremy came with friends from the city for the weekend. We all rode on the old-fashioned train through the woods. Angelina sat next to my friend Phoebe. Later Phoebe told me, "You know, Jeremy's really lucky. Angelina thinks he's a terrific father."

It was hard for Jeremy to know how to deal with Angelina, but there was no question that he knew how to show his love for his children. I was pleased to hear that Angelina recognized this. She was probably as uncomfortable as he was, not quite into a guest role, not quite out of a domestic role. She kept hopping up from the table, doing the dishes, sweeping.

On Sunday morning we went to church in town. I carried Will in the Snugli. Christopher was restless, so Angelina took him outside to play on the stone patio. Coming back from communion, I recognized Chris's screams. I rushed outside to find him lying on the ground. Angelina held a blood-soaked handkerchief to his nose. "I fell off the wall," he sobbed. Angelina appeared to be comatose. I picked up Christopher, now wailing in misery, balanced him against my hip (Will was in the Snugli on my chest), and dragged all three of us across the street to the general store next to the gas station. I asked for ice-filled paper towels, which I held to Chris's nose until the blood stopped. A couple of large scabs were already starting to form.

Another day Christopher and Angelina were playing on the floor in his bedroom. A small, old-fashioned fan whirred on the floor next to them. Somehow Chris managed to get one of his big toes caught in the fan. God knows how it happened, but he yowled like nothing on earth. He wouldn't let Angelina comfort him and yelled at her, "Get out! Get out!"

By the time I got upstairs the nail was blue. Christopher made everyone go downstairs while I rocked him and wrapped his toe in a wet towel. I gave him a fudge ice cream bar to stop the crying. He woke up at about midnight crying in pain, so I let him come in bed with me. Angelina appeared in the hallway outside her door for a moment but retreated to her room when she saw me.

These were fairly typical accidents for a four-year-old. But they both happened when Christopher was alone with Angelina. Could she take care of him? Did these accidents seem abnormal because they happened around her?

The next day I scooped up Will and told my mother to get in the car; we were going out to lunch. Angelina could make something for herself and Christopher. I felt uneasy about leaving Chris out, but I needed to get away from Angelina.

That evening I met Jeremy at a restaurant about twenty minutes from our house. The bus dropped him off; I was waiting with margaritas on the restaurant's outdoor deck. Instead of the pleasant dinner I'd planned, I launched into an attack on him before we had finished our drinks.

"You act like she doesn't exist," I accused Jeremy.

"What do you want me to do?" he said, exasperated.

"Just treat her like a human being. Last weekend you acted like she's the maid. All you have to do is talk to her a little bit."

"She doesn't speak English," he said.

"And I don't speak Spanish," I said. "But we talk."

"About what?"

"About anything, Jeremy. What do you talk about with anyone? The weather, the kids, the swimming hole, the garden."

It was a lousy weekend. Late Sunday morning Jeremy decided to flag down the noon bus and go back to the city early. We'd slept with our backs to each other the night before. He left without saying good-bye to Christopher, who was down at the swimming hole with Angelina.

I felt an oddly similar sense of relief as I watched Angelina's bus pull onto the highway a few days later. Her appointed stay was over and she, too, had to get back to work.

My sister Katherine and her husband, Philip, in New York City on business, drove up to the country with Jeremy the next weekend. They called to say they would stop en route for dinner. When they hadn't arrived by midnight, my mother and I went to bed. About two hours later, I heard stumbling and giggling in the driveway. I pretended to be asleep. The next day Katherine and I had a confidential discussion in the A&P parking lot in town. She said that when she brought up the subject of Angelina at dinner, the drinks had begun to flow. Jeremy told Katherine that it was a "failure of Maggie's intellect to see my position on Angelina."

"A *failure* of the intellect?" I said, sarcastically. "Like he thinks there's something missing, something deficient? A *failure* of the intellect? That's too much!"

Katherine laughed with me, but then she said, "Maggie, it was really strange last night. Jeremy cried and cried. Every time Philip tired to say something, we'd say to him, 'Could you just let us talk, please, Philip?' I must have had five Black Russians. Jeremy must have had five Scotches. I think he feels abandoned, like you've gone over to Angelina's side and don't care about him anymore."

"Oh God," I sighed. "That's ridiculous. He says I have a failure of the intellect because I can't see his position on Angelina? As far as I can see, with this failed intellect, he has no position. I'm getting real tired of doing all the work with Angelina."

"You have to do it," said Katherine.

"Why?" I said sullenly.

"Because you are strong," she said. "Because God has given you the ability to do it. You're lucky, really. You can deal with your pain. Jeremy can't. You should have seen him last night. He loves you. He loves the kids. He needs you. You should have seen him crying."

"I'm sure the crying was partly the Scotch," I said.

"Of course," Katherine agreed. "But the feelings were there. The Scotch just helped them come out. He really needs you. I've known Jeremy for—what—fifteen years?" Katherine said. "He's never acted like this. You guys have been through so much with Christopher. How can any relationship survive so much suffering? I think you're being too hard on Jeremy. He hasn't found any positive way to deal with his pain. I think he really needs you now, Maggie. Don't turn away from him."

"I will try," I said, pulling out of the parking lot.

"What kind of plans are you making for the future, Angelina?" asked Rosa in September.

"Well, I'd like to get an apartment on Long Island. I could take Chris there on weekends. It wouldn't be too far if he cries to come home to Señora Ryan."

"What do you think of that, Maggie?"

"I think it's a good idea to stay in New York." (Alleluia! She's not talking about going back to California anymore!) "Long Island is definitely cheaper than the city." (But how can she take him on weekends? That's when we go to the country.)

"So, you're not planning on California now, Angelina?"

"No, I think it's too far for Chris. I think it's better if he's closer to the Ryans."

"And what about your friend Ramon?"

"Well, he has offered me marriage. He is a good man." (Marriage? Omigod! I wonder if he wants Christopher. Is this the same guy Angelina told my mother about last summer? The one who divorced his wife because they didn't have children?)

"Would you consider marriage?"

"Well." A long pause. "For a long time I lived without any men. Perez, the father of Chris, he tricked me. Everybody told me to be very careful, you know, because of the court case. Sometimes men were interested in me, the man who holds the door at the apartment building. I always said no. But I think Ramon likes the boy."

"Does Ramon want to have children?"

"Yes, I think he does."

(Their own? Christopher? Both?)

"Well, what do you think about this, Maggie?" (What the hell can I think? I hope she marries the guy and they have a thousand kids and leave Chrisopher alone. I'll throw her a shower.)

Rosa put pressure on Angelina to reach a decision. When would she assume custody? How would she provide for Christopher? What was her plan? Rosa worked in a clinic where situations were resolved, decisions were reached, case folders were closed and filed away. Our case was ongoing; the status quo was the best resolution for us. Angelina had spent several years living with American families of a certain wealth. She had a lovely room, nice clothes, good food, people who thought highly of her and treated her well because she took good care of their homes and children. It would be difficult, perhaps impossible, for her to find her own place to live and provide for Christopher.

In one of our final visits with Rosa, Angelina said she'd like to have Christopher spend Christmas with her at the Liebermans. The family was going to Michigan and would permit her to bring Chris to Fifth Avenue. Our plans, however, were for my sister Helen and her husband and three children to come up from Miami to spend ten days with us, part in the Catskills and part in the city. I thought perhaps the best approach to Angelina's plan was simply to go along with it without specifics and see what happened when Christmas week actually rolled around.

At this point, I didn't think we needed to see Rosa every week. I had to hire a babysitter for Will, take the subway up to Columbia Presbyterian, pay thirty dollars for my half of the session (Angelina paid, too). We didn't have that much to talk about now. I thought it would be better to reserve Rosa for irregularly scheduled sessions or special conferences.

The Monday before Christmas Angelina made her usual visit. She had decided it would be too lonely for Christopher and her on Fifth Avenue. She thought Chris should go to the Catskills with us. Delighted, I invited her to join us, but she said she might visit her friends on Long Island. Jeremy and my brother-in-law and two nephews and Christopher and Angelina went to see the latest sequel to *Star Wars* while my sister and I stayed home with our babies.

"She's really kind of nice," said my sister Helen. "I still think my original idea would be a great solution. Angelina can live with you as an au pair. She'd be close to Christopher; you'd have help with the kids; everyone would be happy."

"Yeah, sure," I said, "Jeremy would love it. I can just see him trying to get her a green card. I don't think we could afford her anyway. She makes about ten thousand dollars a year."

"Maybe you wouldn't have to pay her so much," said Helen. "After all, isn't she sort of family?"

In the spring, Angelina continued to visit most Mondays. Christopher went to nursery school only until noon on Mondays, so they were able to spend long afternoons together. Sometimes we four—Angelina, Chris, Will, and I—would go to the park several blocks away. Afterward we might stop in a little cafe for hot chocolate, or shop for some special treat—such as out-of-season raspberries—at a fancy grocery store in the Village. A few times Christopher and Angelina went off to a matinee—*Pinocchio*, *101 Dalmations*. I'd draw a map for Angelina, advising her which bus or subway to take, or suggesting that a taxi would be easiest. After a while, I stopped making suggestions and let them decide together what they would do. Usually they stayed home. Occasionally they would go to Macy's to buy Chris sneakers or a transformer toy.

Angelina seemed to want to integrate herself more into our household. She offered to help with the never-ending domestic chores—vacuuming, folding laundry, emptying the dishwasher. She sat on the floor and played with Will. Once she offered to stay late on a Monday night "if you and Mr. Ryan wan going to restaurant." I accepted eagerly. When we came home, Angelina was sitting on the couch in the children's darkened room. I had expected her to be down in the living room watching television.

In June I invited Angelina to join us at Christopher's graduation from nursery school. She looked very pretty. She wore a white cotton blouse, a black and white striped slim skirt, white stockings, and black pumps. She knew it was a dress-up occasion. But she looked tired, weary, sort of rundown.

Jeremy, Angelina, and I walked together into the large loft of the nursery school (Will, almost recovered from chicken pox, stayed home with a sitter). Small children's chairs were arranged on either side of the central area. Jeremy headed for the far side; Angelina had already sat down in the rear row of the area near the door. I followed

Jeremy, but I was torn. Angelina should sit with us. We were there to see the same child graduate, we were "family." We should have sat together. I felt uneasy.

The children sang—off-key, of course—danced around the Maypole, colliding with one another as their ribbons twisted, then sobered up to receive their diplomas. The director was quite formal, calling out each child's full name, no nicknames, and handing each purple-and-white-capped child his or her diploma with a firm handshake. "Congratulations. Take your diploma to your parents." Christopher headed radarlike for us. I marveled that there had never been any doubt in his mind. I wondered, though, how Angelina felt when the director called out "Christopher Ryan." Did she say to herself, "Lorenzo Rodriguez"? I wrestled between pride for Chris and empathy for Angelina.

Angelina put a chicken wing on Chris's paper plate and filled a glass with orange juice. "My mom made this," I heard him say proudly as he and a friend chomped on their chicken. I filled another plate with raw carrots and broccoli, tabuli and pasta salad, cheese crackers, and more chicken, and slid it in front of Chris. Angelina had taken her food back to the faraway seating area. No one else sat there. All the parents and grandparents crowded around the food table and chattered.

"Where's Christopher going for kindergarten?"

"Karen will go to day camp this summer on Fire Island."

"When do you leave for the Catskills?"

"Is that soy sauce on the chicken? Can I have the recipe? Annie had three pieces and she hates chicken."

"Our cleaning lady gave the baby Coke in his bottle!"

"I hope the pictures turn out—Seth never sits still."

"Did you know that forty kids have registered at Little Red Schoolhouse for kindergarten?"

I was entrenched in parent talk. The children had finished their lunches and were running around the May-pole, popping balloons. Angelina sat with her hands in her lap in a child's chair, waiting until someone said it was time to go.

Andrew's mother came up to me and said, "Who is that girl over there with Christopher? A babysitter?"

"Well, no," I said, "she's a friend of the family."

"Does Chris speak Spanish?" she asked. "Because I heard her speaking Spanish to him."

"Oh, just a few words," I said.

"I asked her in Spanish who she was and she said 'part of the family.' "

"Yes," I said, "she's a friend."

She wanted to say more but instead decided on, "OK, I gotta get back to work. Have a good summer."

Jeremy came up and said he had heard the woman next to him whispering to her husband and pointing at Ange-lina. He heard her say, "Doesn't that just make you sick?"

"What do you think she meant?" I said.

"I don't know," he answered.

"Well, she substituted for a teacher one week and the director might have told her the whole story," I said. "But she's probably on our side, don't you think?"

"I don't know," Jeremy repeated.

It is tiring not to be a plain, normal parent. My guard is always up. That cold familiar feeling in my stomach returns so quickly.

Christopher and Angelina spent the afternoon of the graduation at the movies. When Angelina brought him home, she seemed subdued, quieter than usual. I told her we planned to spend the summer in the Catskills; she was welcome to come. She was vague, uncertain, said she'd call.

Rosa Levano phoned the next morning. "Maggie, I felt that I had to call you. I am violating the confidentiality of a client, but I'm going to do it anyway."

"Rosa, what's happening?"

"Angelina called me last week. She said she was having some trouble with her eyes and she wondered whether I could get her into the clinic up here. I had to cut through a lot of red tape to do it, because she does live on Fifth Avenue, and with an address like that, you usually don't apply to our clinic. Anyway, I got her an appointment and told her to stop by at my office later. She seemed very nervous and upset, like she did last spring, and she finally said that she had decided to take Christopher with her to California. She was going to do it without telling you because she couldn't bring herself to tell you. She was going to take him out for the afternoon and not bring him back."

Rosa stopped. There was a short silence. "My God," I said.

"We talked for a while and I managed to calm her down a bit and asked her how she thought that would affect Christopher. She promised to think carefully about it after she left my office. This morning she called and said she had decided not to take him yet. She told her friend Ramon about her plan and he told her it was a very bad idea. He told her not to snatch him away, but maybe to try to have him for a week this summer."

"I thought she was acting strange at Chris's graduation yesterday," I said. "But planning to take him without telling me? Or telling *him*?"

"Maggie, I'm sure she's afraid of your reaction. She said to me, 'Mrs. Ryan has a husband, two children, her church, two houses. She's in control of so many things and I can't even control one.' She was crying."

"I did tell her we'd be away for two months," I said. "That was probably a dumb thing to do. But I invited her to come, like last summer."

"Obviously, she made her own plans," said Rosa. "But I think she's calmed down now. Ramon talked some sense into her. Also, I think she likes the idea of ventilating to me. But I really shouldn't be telling you any of this."

"Rosa, you had to tell me," I said. "Actually, every time Christopher goes out with Angelina, I have a fear that he might not come back. I get very anxious if he's late. But think of how terrified *he* would be if she didn't bring him back."

"I think Ramon helped convince her of that," said Rosa.

"Thank God for Ramon," I said.

When Angelina came over the next afternoon, she made no mention of her plan. I told her we'd be leaving for just two *weeks* in the Catskills and would then come back to the city so she could visit. She asked me whether I thought Christopher would spend some time with her at the Liebermans. They would be away for a few weeks and she had to maintain the apartment, water the plants, collect the mail, feed the dog. I told her to ask Christopher herself.

"Chris, you wan coming with me to Fifth Avenue?"

"No."

"Why not?"

"Because I want to be with Mom."

"OK," she sighed, "I call you in Catskills."

Jeremy stayed with us in the country the whole two weeks. We celebrated Will's first birthday. Will at one was sheer energy, movement from the moment he awoke until he collapsed for a nap. Comparing photographs of Christopher and Will on their first birthdays is interesting. Chris is nestled in Jeremy's arms, smiling into the camera, tranquil, content. Will is trying to squirm out of my arms, limbs flailing, mouth open, looking off somewhere else. He was still basically bald, with only a few wisps of blond hair. When Chris was one I had to give him a major haircut so he could see. I filled a baggie with his hair and a friend later stuffed a toy bear with it.

An early walker, Will was into everything. Wearing only a diaper, he toddled through the field of daisies, his chunky legs moving at great speed, to chase Christopher, who was proudly riding his two-wheeler without its training wheels. "Kiss, Kiss" (his version of Chris), Will yelled after him. Christopher would stop and give his brother a kiss.

Jeremy built an enormous wooden sandbox for the boys; Chris and I painted it forest green. While Jeremy and I planted a garden, Chris pushed Will around in the wheelbarrow. Chris went on every ride at the Fourth of July Firemen's Carnival and was introduced to fireworks and cotton candy.

I forgot all about Angelina until she phoned one afternoon while Will was napping and Jeremy and Christopher were down at the river fishing for trout. I told her we'd be back in the city, expecting her visit, the next Monday morning. "Chris wan coming with me?" she asked again.

"You'll have to ask him yourself," I replied.

I hated going back to the city, trading our pastoral existence—the river, cool spruce trees, picnics, wildflowers, barbecues. "The air smells yuck," said Christopher as we exited the Lincoln Tunnel.

Angelina phoned Monday morning. Did I think Chris would come with her? I repeated that he continued to say no, and she said, "OK, I come over for a few hours. Maybe he wan coming tomorrow."

She arrived just before noon. We chatted a little, then I left her to play with Christopher in his room. Will was napping in his crib in our bedroom and I was folding laundry in the living room when Chris came running down to me, crying, "Mom, Angelina said she wants to take me to her house. Please, Mom, I don't want to go."

What is she trying to pull, I thought to myself. We had talked about tomorrow. Of course I never expected Christopher to agree to go.

"OK, Chris, OK." I hugged him. "You don't have to go."

"Tell her, Mom. You tell her."

Angelina strolled into the living room, regarded the piles of laundry, said, "Everything ready?"

"For what?"

"Chris coming with me today."

"I thought you said tomorrow."

"No, is necessary going today."

"Hold me, Mom," said Christopher in a strained, high-pitched voice. I wasn't sure whether Angelina wanted to take him for a visit or *what*.

Chris's crying woke Will. He started crying, too. I carried Christopher into our bedroom and lifted Will from his crib. The two of them must have weighed sixty-five pounds together. I sat down on our bed. Angelina sat down, too.

"Is necessary going today," she said. "Chris almost five years old."

"Angelina," I said. "I know it's very hard for you. You love Chris. But he's afraid of you now." Christopher clung to me. The buzzer on the clothes dryer went off. It buzzes loudly for over a minute, so I didn't want to wait for it to go off by itself. I started to walk out of the bedroom carrying Will. "Mom, don't leave me," cried Chris in a terrified voice. I carried them both with me to turn the dryer off. I hoped I wouldn't drop Will.

Angelina trailed behind me. "Chris, put your shoes on. We going now." I had never seen her this determined, this driven. She had given herself a deadline.

"Mom, please, Mom," wailed Christopher. He ran to me and hung onto my legs. Angelina picked up his sneakers and pulled at him. "Maggie," she said, "please press the elevator button. Chris, is not California, is Fifth Avenue. You call Maggie every day in Catskills." Will looked back and forth from Angelina to me, uncertain of what was happening, interested in the tones of our voices. Chris clawed at me to pick him up.

Angelina pushed the elevator button, and when the door opened, she backed in, pulling on Christopher, who was still hanging on my bare legs. Chris screamed, "*Help me, Mom!*" Angelina pulled, wailing, "Please, please." I hesitated for a second, but I had no choice. My child was drowning and I held his lifeline. I stepped backward, pulling Chris and Angelina forward. The elevator door slammed shut. We all stood still for a moment, frozen, then Angelina retreated into Christopher's room. Chris, Will, and I stood in the kitchen.

I went in to her, sitting on the couch, staring down at the carpet. "Angelina, I know you love Chris. It's very hard for you. But he's only a little boy; he doesn't understand. What good will it do to hurt him?" She looked up at me; I could see the resentment in her eyes, but I had to finish. "I couldn't let him go, Angelina. He has to know I love him, too." She looked back down at the floor and didn't say anything. My heart was pounding.

"I have to get Will some lunch now," I said. All this drama had bypassed him, and he was hungry.

I didn't know what to do. I called Theo, but her answering machine was on. I left a message for her to call me immediately and fed Will some soup, yogurt, a bottle of milk. Christopher stood as close to me as possible during the meal. When he saw that Angelina wasn't going to try anything, he calmed down. He asked for a piece of paper so Angelina could write down the things he wanted for his birthday—Batman pajamas, GoBots.

Theo called. I wanted to go up to her, but Christopher wouldn't let me leave, so I asked her to come down, telling her briefly what had happened. She stepped out of the elevator and greeted everyone cheerily. "Angelina, how are you? Are you coming to the mountains this summer?"

"I wan Chris coming with me but he afraid," said Angelina. She started to cry.

"Maggie, I'm taking Angelina upstairs with me," said Theo. They disappeared into the elevator. I kept watching the clock, feeling that the longer Angelina stayed with Theo, the better. Chris got out the record that my sister had sent for his birthday, "Hey, Chris, It's Your Birthday," and Will and Chris and I danced around the living room.

When Theo and Angelina came back downstairs about an hour later, Theo told me to sit down at the kitchen table. She pulled out a chair for Angelina, then one for herself.

"We are going to talk," she announced. "Angelina, do you want to see more of Christopher?"

"Yes."

"Then say so. When are your days off?"

"Sunday and Monday."

"Do you want to see Christopher on Sunday and Monday?"

"Yes."

"Then say so."

"I wan see Christopher Sunday and Monday."

"Maggie," asked Theo, "is that all right with you?"

"Yes," I replied, "anything is possible."

With Theo leading us, we could communicate. I winced looking at Angelina, hearing the echo of her primal scream and seeing her animal look when she had tried to pull Christopher into the elevator with her.

"Angelina, you must be tired. Go home now," said Theo. "You'll call tomorrow, right?"

After Angelina had gone, Theo said, "She cried and cried. She hugged me. She was planning on taking Christopher to the Liebermans for two weeks, then leaving for California with him. She had already given notice."

"Really," I said, stunned. "What did she say?"

"She's like a horse with blinders on—Christopher, Christopher, Christopher. She eats, sleeps, dreams Christopher. She can't do anything else until she gets him. She thinks if she can get him to go with her, then she can get on with her life. I told her that Christopher isn't ready to go with her. But I also told her he's very lucky because she loves him so much. I told her he's beginning to love her, too."

"What did she say to that?" I asked.

"She just kept crying," said Theo. "I told her that Christopher is just a small part of her life. I told her he's going to grow up fast and not even have time for her. I told her it's not enough for her to say to him, 'I want you to come with me.' I told her she has to improve her English. I told her she needed some men in her life, that she should have another baby. 'Look at what a beautiful child you made,' I said. 'Why don't you have another one?' I asked about her boyfriend Ramon. She said

Ramon complains that she doesn't love him back. Then she said, 'I quit my job. Would you call Mrs. Lieberman and see if I can get my job back?' "

"Did you call her?"

"Yes," said Theo. "She told me they love Angelina, she always has a home with them. Mrs. Lieberman said that she thinks it's a horrendous situation and her family has tried to stay out of it. They are somewhat ambivalent about the ending because they don't think it would be such a good idea for her to go to California with Christopher. But she wants to know whether Angelina is leaving, because she'll have to get another girl. Angelina is their employee, you know, it's her job."

"So you got her job back for her?" I said. "That's great; that's amazing." I was overcome with gratitude and relief.

The next morning Angelina called and asked for Christopher without greeting me first. She always talked with me first. I stood near Chris so I could hear what he said to her. Holding the phone tightly in his little hand, he said, "No, I have a sore throat. Call tomorrow." Then he hung up. I made him call her back to ask about the birthday party plans. She was cool with me, saying only, "I'll call you tomorrow, OK?"

This evasive behavior made me nervous. Jeremy called Jeffrey Laef, our appeals lawyer. Jeffrey said that if Angelina tried to take Christopher and we resisted, we would be in contempt of court. He gave Jeremy two examples of clients in contempt of court. One was a woman who refused to disclose the whereabouts of her child; she was in jail on Rikers Island. Another was a client in contempt of court who had been walking the streets freely for three years. Jeffrey's advice was that we take a vacation, thereby avoiding any action on Angelina's part. I was surprised and dismayed that Jeffrey would propose—and Jeremy would consider—such a tactic at this highly sensitive stage. I'd been working hard to secure Angelina's trust; it didn't seem right to consider running now.

I asked Rosa to call Angelina. Angelina told her she was still planning on taking Christopher to California in two weeks. Rosa, on vacation, volunteered to come down to our house to meet with me and Angelina. When Angelina phoned as promised at eleven, Christopher told her he still had a sore throat. He suggested that she call the next day. I interjected, "Tell her to come today, Chris. You don't have to go out if you don't want to."

He looked at me, considered, then said grudgingly into the receiver, "OK, come today." I took the phone and asked Angelina whether it was all right with her if Rosa came over to talk. She agreed. Angelina was due to arrive at 2:30; Rosa, at 3:00. When Will awoke from his nap, I told Chris to climb in his crib with him to keep him happy while I finished vacuuming. Everything looked terrific when Angelina arrived. Theo came down shortly after to take the boys out for a walk so we could arbitrate in peace. When Rosa arrived, she and Angelina talked a long while in Spanish.

Angelina seemed to have reached a resolution. She was concerned about Christopher; she didn't want him to get sick. She would leave him with us. She used the word *resigned* a lot. She looked very, very sad, quite pale, strained. Her grief was palpable. She was trying hard not to cry. She said, "If it make Chris sick to see me, I stay away. If the telephone bother him, I no call."

"He likes you to visit," I said. "He really looks forward to Mondays. But he's afraid now. He thought of you as a friend for a long time, a big friend. Then he had to get used to the idea of your giving birth to him. The idea of California is terrifying to him."

Rosa translated. Angelina listened carefully, gnawing with her teeth at her lower lip.

"I would like him to hear that I am his mother," she said. Apparently, when she had told him that she was his real mother, he had been adamant. "NO. Mom is my real mom."

"We'd love to have you visit us in the Catskills," I said.

Angelina answered maybe. She wanted to leave us alone there. "She recognizes that you are an intact family," Rosa said.

I respected Angelina because obviously she valued herself enough not to take Christopher if he did not want to be with her. Her loving Chris meant that she wanted him to be happy. If his being happy meant being with us, then she would step aside. Her disappointment and her feeling of loss were painfully evident. She was grieving as if there had been a death. Her pain was my pain.

"Maybe we could talk about Chris's birthday party," I said, trying to lighten the gloom. The buzzer sounded; Chris and Will were back, their faces and hands sticky with Italian ice. Christopher ran into the living room and squeezed himself next to me on the corner of the couch away from Angelina.

"Would you like to have your birthday party here, Chris?" I said.

"In the country," he said, "a picnic."

"Well, maybe we could have it here so Angelina can come."

"OK," he sighed, resigned.

Angelina suggested pizza and just children for guests, no grownups. I wondered whether we'd be able to round up any guests on such short notice in the middle of July. So many children from Christopher's nursery school went away in the summer—Annie to her grandparents in Italy, Francois and Pascal to their relatives in France.

Angelina said she would like to ask Christopher one more question, down in his room. They got up together and disappeared. Angelina came back to the living room a minute or so later, confessing that she'd asked him whether he would go with her one day. His response had been, "Maybe when I'm six."

Everyone stood up to leave. The crisis was over. I thanked Rosa and Theo, said good-bye to Angelina, then called Jeremy to report. The boys and I went to the deli to buy a quart of milk. "How's that sore throat?" I asked Chris.

"Mom, you know what?" he said. "I was just pretending I had a sore throat so Angelina could understand better."

I stopped to hug him then and there. "Christopher Ryan," I said, "you are an amazing boy."

"Does that mean I can get a soda?" he said.

Under the influence of a few glasses of white wine later that evening, I told Christopher to call Angelina. I got on the phone and said to her, "I love you, Angelina. You're so strong." She probably thought I was crazy. A little later, watching television, I said to him, "Christopher, you're a wonderful boy, do you know that?"

His response: "Angelina understands better now, right, Mom?"

Angelina came over the next Monday, the day before Christopher's birthday party. She seemed her usual self, not upset at all. I said I might go grocery shopping with Will. Christopher said we should all go or he and I should go and Angelina could stay home with Will. He was clearly afraid to be alone with her. Angelina said if we went out, she'd go home. I thought to myself, All I want to do is go to the A&P. How much longer can this craziness go on? Will I be a Monday prisoner for the rest of my life?

Theo came down. She chatted breezily with Angelina. "You're so thin. . . . Your hair looks great short like that. . . . It's so hot; do the Liebermans have central air conditioning?" Angelina smiled, responded. I felt better, too. Theo had the knack. Angelina and Christopher decided to go out for pizza and were back in sixteen minutes, a new speed record.

Angelina came early for the party. Chris's greeting to her was, "Did you get the Batman pajamas?" She had, of course, done as she had been told. Angelina helped blow up balloons and give Christopher a bath.

Andrew said to Chris, "Who's that over there, Chris, your babysitter?"

"You mean that lady over there?" Chris said. "She's a friend." I hoped Angelina hadn't heard this exchange.

When she left, Angelina said to me, "You don't have to come home next Sunday or Monday. I call you in Catskills."

A few days later, when we were walking down by the river, out of the blue Christopher said to me, "Mom, what did Theo say to Angelina? What did Mrs. Levano say? It's a good thing Theo and Mrs. Levano went to school to find out how to help people with problems."

I tried to be straight with Christopher about what was happening. "Angelina has no money. Her family lives in El Salvador, a country where almost everyone is poor. There is a war going on there, people fighting each other with guns all the time. Angelina wanted you to have a good home with both a mommy and a daddy. Then she changed her mind and wanted to take you away to California. We love you too much to let you go with her. We never want you to go with Angelina. We always want you to live with us and Will."

"Me, too. I know," said Chris, "maybe someday you and Dad and Will and me will go to California for a trip and Angelina can come, too."

Seventeen

Almost two years have passed since that exchange between Christopher and me. He is in first grade now, the best reader in his class. His teacher says he's a joy to have as a student, a role model for the other children. In the city he watches too much television and takes forever to go to bed at night. In the country he swims, rides horseback, skis, and falls asleep early.

Christopher and Will are very different from each other. Not just physically—Chris is dark and lean, Will is blond and sturdy—but also temperamentally. Christopher tends to be shy, inward, serious. Will is all up front, a tornado of energy and emotions from morning until night. Christopher is protective, calmly tolerant, of his little brother, and Will adores Chris.

They relate to each other like all brothers. That is, they fight, sometimes with words, sometimes with slaps and pinches, over everything. Ten minutes later they're snuggled on the couch while Chris reads to Will. "Will is, you know," says Chris, raising his eyebrows and shrugging his shoulders, "a little wild."

Will is a funny child. He struts about with his chest stuck out like a bantam rooster. The first day of nursery school, when other little boys and girls clung to their mothers' legs, Will barely remembered to say good-bye, he was so excited about all the other two-year-olds. Early on in the school year, he appointed himself official chronicler of decorum, so that his monologue on the way home would go something like this: "Mama, you know what? Alex was naughty today. Teresa made him sit in the office. I don't like Matthew. I mean the little Matthew, not the big one. He bites."

A second later, without waiting for my response, "Lara didn't eat her lunch. She doesn't like peanut butter anymore."

"And what did you do today, Will?"

"Oh, nothing. Did you bring me a treat, Mama? Oh, could we get some gum, then? The pink kind, without sugar? Should we pick up Dad's shirts at the laundry? Oh, Mama, let's walk on the other side of the street. I like shady. Where's Chris? Oh, still at school? Can we pick him up after my nap? Can we get ice cream?"

Sometimes the traffic on Broadway is so loud that I can't hear what he's saying, and I'll periodically mutter down into the stroller, "That's nice, Will." Or I'll issue one of my frequent deep sighs and Will says, "Who's bothering you now, Mama?"

Will's energy level is so high that luckily he still collapses for a two-hour nap every afternoon. Sometimes when he naps, I sit down and simply breathe in and out for several seconds, mesmerized by the quiet.

One major difference between our two children is that Will sings on car trips and Christopher doesn't. Driving along a local country road, Will and I crank out "She'll

Be Comin' 'Round the Mountain'' while Christopher buries his nose in a video game the size of a matchbook, intermittent sonic beep-beeps his only sign of consciousness.

In fact, Will is such an ebullient, precocious, attention-grabbing little charmer that Jeremy and I worry somewhat about Christopher's ego. We began "Special Time" about two years ago. Jeremy tries to take at least one afternoon off from work every two weeks. He picks Chris up from school and they head off on an exclusive father-and-son excursion. They share a passion for science fiction movies that only a seven-year-old boy and his father could enjoy, ones with titles like *Project X*, or *Poltergeist*. They've been to most of Jeremy's construction sites; Christopher has his own hard hat (it's purple). After they went several times to a laser-generated computer show in a midtown office building, Grandpa Ryan sent us a computer. Christopher has generously offered to teach me to use it.

Almost without noticing it, Jeremy and I had come to the point where we touched each other less and less, and this physical nontouching was coupled with an emotional remoteness. Our relationship was withering. I didn't seem to have time for him after expending my efforts on the children.

Over the Fourth of July holiday in the country last summer, Jeremy suddenly began suffering a severe, continuous headache. A local doctor prescribed antiobiotics for what he diagnosed as a sinus condition. The headache continued. Back in the city, Jeremy's internist suspected meningitis but couldn't convince Jeremy to enter the hospital. In the country the next weekend, the headache intensified, and periods of heavy sweating alternated with chills so severe that our iron bed shook at night.

My mother and I finally persuaded Jeremy to go into the hospital. The children were strapped into their car seats on either side of my mother in the backseat, and Jeremy slumped in the front passenger seat while I chased our two chickens, incubated in Christopher's kindergarten class during May and June, around the barn in vain. Unable to catch them, I phoned a neighbor, who promised to care for the chickens until we returned. Jeremy dozed, moaning now and then, on the long drive home.

We had to wait two days for Jeremy to be admitted, during which time his doctor took him off medication so that his system would be pure for testing. When he got up from bed to go to the bathroom, he lost his sense of balance and crashed into our bedroom wall. Subdued by his father's condition, Christopher tiptoed around the loft, but Will, only two, was oblivious to his father's pain and remained his usual boisterous self, nearly driving us crazy while we waited for the phone to ring and a voice to say that a hospital bed was available. At least Jeremy kept cool in our air-conditioned bedroom. He wouldn't eat but drank enormous quantities of iced ginger ale.

Moments after the hospital phoned, I had a cab waiting downstairs. Jeremy sagged against me, his fresh shirt already soaked with sweat, on the drive to the hospital. My mother stayed home with the children.

During his first twelve hours in the hospital, Jeremy was seen by a neurologist and an infectious disease specialist as well as his internist. He was given a CAT scan, an echocardiogram, and a spinal tap. The doctors were baffled, anxious to see cultures grown from blood tests taken almost two weeks earlier by the internist. They couldn't pinpoint his illness but now entertained hepatitis as well as meningitis.

"*Six weeks!*" Jeremy said incredulously to his doctor. "WHAT?"

"Six weeks of intravenous antibotics," replied the doctor calmly. "Standard procedure."

"Can I take this medication as an outpatient?" asked Jeremy.

"Absolutely not," said the doctor.

"Jeremy," I said, "are you crazy? Imagine rattling around your office hooked up to an IV pole. Running back and forth to the hospital eight times a day to have the needle taken in or out? Getting in a taxi with that pole?"

The doctor laughed. "Make yourself comfortable," he said to Jeremy. "This will be home for a while."

"What I need in this IV," said Jeremy, "is a Scotch."

"My mom and I will have one for you tonight," I assured him.

Among them, the doctors finally diagnosed Jeremy's illness as endocarditis, an infection of the lining of the heart. Jeremy had been told about five years earlier that he had a heart click, a minor condition that affects about 5 percent of the population. Somehow over the past several weeks, possibly at a seemingly innocuous dental visit, bacteria had entered his bloodstream and worn down a heart valve. Because of Jeremy's imbalance and double vision when he entered the hospital, the neurologist suspected that the infection had traveled into the cerebrum, the center of balance, in the brain. The neurologist ordered an angiogram, threading a microscopic needle from the thigh up into the brain, injecting dye to read the cranial arteries. When Jeremy was wheeled back on a stretcher from his test, his hair was covered with a shower cap and his forehead was bloody and bruised. He said he wanted to nap and had dozed off when the neurologist came in the room.

Jeremy had a small aneurism in a brain artery, the neurologist said, like the swelling in an inner tube. He hoped the aneurism would heal itself during the six weeks in the hospital. Sometimes, he said, an aneurism might burst and fill the brain with blood. His calm, deliberate manner filled me with panic.

While Jeremy slept, I raced down to the hospital library to look up heart infections, aneurisms. A heart valve replacement? Brain surgery? The more I read, the more scared I got. I thought Jeremy might die and I saw myself—a single mother with two small children. I felt afraid. Then I felt guilty. I went back to Jeremy's room, deciding not to tell him all the details of my conversation with the neurologist. When he awoke, I poured him ice water and told him my plan—to go around the block and bring him back some Chinese food for dinner.

I downplayed the aneurism, focusing on the neurologist's intention to repeat the angiogram before Jeremy was released from the hospital. It would most likely be healed, we figured.

The six weeks passed almost pleasantly. Jeremy remained in his four-bed room, outstaying twenty-four roommates, including one who died in his bed. During those six weeks, Jeremy had needle-free wrists only about two hours a day. He never complained.

Outside, the August heat blazed. Angelina had planned to spend her two-week vacation in the Catskills with us. Instead she came down to Soho almost every day, slept over a few nights, took the children to the park, chatted with my mother. This freed me to spend most of my waking hours at the hospital. For the first few weeks, when he was weak and barely able to walk, I bathed Jeremy, soaping his body, washing his hair, rinsing him, helping him step into his pajama pants. When the food tray came, I poured his milk, cut his meat. "I'm just like the kids," he said. His frailty and dependence endeared him to me.

Jeremy and I spent more time talking than we had in months. I'd talk about the kids, how Will knocked the television off its stand when he crashed into it with his minicar. How Christopher charmed my mother into buying five frozen pizzas at the grocery store. How the entire half of my closet shelving collapsed when I overloaded it. How our friend Tom came in from Connecticut, fixed the television, rehung the closet rods, and took everybody to the South Street Seaport for lunch. I elaborated on the details of these stories, Jeremy's laughter was my reward.

We talked about his business, some hopes and concerns he had that I'd never known about. Maybe I hadn't listened. I brought him cheeseburgers from the local bar, Moussy (non-alcoholic beer) from the deli, milkshakes from the hospital cafeteria, wildflowers and handmade pretzels from the Farmer's Market. The children weren't allowed in Jeremy's ward, but we strolled in nonchalantly a few times, collected Jeremy, and went out into the lounge. No one complained. Christopher was allowed to work the levers on the hospital bed and was impressed with the food trays and the fact that Jeremy could have chocolate milk with every meal.

My mother took the children to Chicago to a family reunion we'd all planned on attending. Surrounded by sixty aunts, uncles, and cousins, Christopher and Will were in heaven.

"I want to write a will," Jeremy said one afternoon. "I've been thinking about it for years, and I've got the time now." His plans for the children were innovative. Christopher was an heir depending on the condition that if he were living with Angelina, he would have to be kept in contact with Will in order for him to receive his due.

In church the next Sunday, I was stunned to hear "Jeremy Ryan" named in the prayers for the sick. I realized how lucky we all were that he had come through. I felt tenderness for him, an awareness, a fresh respect.

Jeremy is healthy now. The aneurism has healed. His heart isn't as strong as it could be, but he is careful with his body and his cardiologist is optimistic. His illness brought us back together in the way that only a crisis can. "I couldn't have gotten through this without you," Jeremy said. That was good for me to hear. It made me realize that he needed me. I certainly need him.

Recently I recorded some medical information in Christopher's baby book and read for the first time what Jeremy had written under the section titled "Father's Message to Baby." "I want you to live long and well. Life should be lived, not in the middle areas, but on the superlative edges—longest, sweetest, in the best sense. I want you to have the ability to make decisions (again in the superlative) and the presence to live those decisions." I sat for several minutes absorbing those words. Jeremy had the courage to make the decision to fight for Christopher in the first place. He took the chances, gambled, wagered for what he believed in. Jeremy's wish for Christopher was to live with integrity, as Jeremy himself lived.

Angelina remains. She comes on Mondays. She trusts me now. Our interests are not at odds. She sees me as an ally; we are joined together for the common purpose of loving Christopher.

She has just as much power as I do. But I can't give it to her. She has to claim it.

For example, I always pick up Christopher from school on Mondays. I have to awaken Will from his nap, and he's often grouchy, dawdling. We dash off to Chris's school, then rush home, where Angelina waits on the street. It would be much simpler for me if Angelina picked up Christopher. But it would establish a precedent on my part, a letting go. It would also present her with the perfect opportunity to pick him up and not bring him back without having to face me. I doubt she would do that, but how do I know for sure?

Will she come over on Mondays for the next ten years? Christopher will be seventeen then, graduating from high school. I envision an Ivy League college, Yale or Harvard, not too far from us for weekend visits.

A few days ago I asked Christopher if he plans to get married when he grows up. *"Hmmm,"* he said thoughtfully, "I don't think so. I think I'll just stay with you and Dad. But I'll be a teacher then, so I won't be home too much, just half the time. And then I can do what I want because I'll be a grownup."

I'm cautious, a little manipulative. Once I asked him if he might ever want to live with Angelina and he said, "What would you want me to do?" I said, "I always want you to live with Daddy and Will and me. This is your home; you don't have to go." When Angelina speculates with me about whether Christopher might spend a week with her next summer, I empathize, saying, "I know how hard it must be for you."

I don't really want to know Angelina's plans for the future. She must have hopes and dreams about Christopher in order to keep on living. She seems entrenched in her Fifth Avenue family, especially since the arrival of a new baby a year ago. Perhaps the new immigration amnesty law will change her ambition. Once she mentioned going to a lawyer to get her papers in order. Her mother died about a year ago in El Salvador. When she told me I cried. I felt so sorry for both of them. They hadn't seen each other for eight years, and Angelina had been thinking about a trip home. I imagined how hurt her mother must have been by what had happened to her daughter.

Angelina is a decent woman. Sometimes I feel very close to her. I think about her all the time. I hold imaginary conversations with her. Sometimes when I buy something for myself I want to get her one, too. I am confused about this coming Sunday, Mother's Day. Should we stay in the city so she can spend Sunday with Christopher? She politely offers, "Why not go to Catskills? It might be beautiful weekend." She thinks of what is best for Christopher.

Christopher is where he belongs. I believe that. I know, too, that troubled dreams lie ahead for him. We'll probably need help to deal with his pain, anger, and confusion. It's easier to live with your birth parents, not to be adopted, not to feel ambivalent about your biological mother. He'll have questions about Will's biological mother. We'll have to work through the answers together, all of us.

Fortunately, my pain has been an agent for transformation. I have reconciled with the church, returned to a sense of a personal God. My alienation began to dissolve when I discovered that the Christian story as lived in my community was my own story. With this realization comes a sense of responsibility for Angelina. Jeremy and I are happy with Christopher. He is happy with us. The one left out is Angelina, and I blame myself for her pain. What can I do to release her? Can a child have two mothers?

Christopher is growing—his interests range from dinosaurs to computers. He is patient with Angelina, slowly repeating the rules of his increasingly complicated games. He's given Candyland to Will and acquired Monopoly and Clue.

In her simplicity and endurance toward him, Angelina has demonstrated a formidable strength of character. Her letting go to let him grow, her fluidity regarding his freedom, is a true measure of love. I am proud of her, proud of his heritage. Maybe the day will come when I can let others know I value her, give her public affirmation: "This is Angelina, Christopher's other mother." I feel an obligation to be a healing channel for her, to break down barriers and make her more integrated with us, less estranged.

"How can you stand it?" a friend once asked me. "I couldn't bear the uncertainty."

"We love him" was my response, "and he loves us."

There is no independent present. The past has been woven in, absorbed, but I try to be free of it. Along with regrets come expectations. Our future with Christopher will be a challenge, filled with unknowns but fortified with glorious possibilities.